CAPE BRETON ISLAND

CAPE BRETON ISLAND

by JIM and PAT LOTZ

Douglas, David & Charles, Vancouver

Douglas, David & Charles
3645 McKechnie Drive
West Vancouver, British Columbia

ISBN 0-88914-018-9
73 74 75 76 77 5 4 3 2 1

Printed in Great Britain by
Latimer Trend & Company Ltd

CONTENTS

ILLUSTRATIONS

ILLUSTRATIONS

ILLUSTRATIONS

9

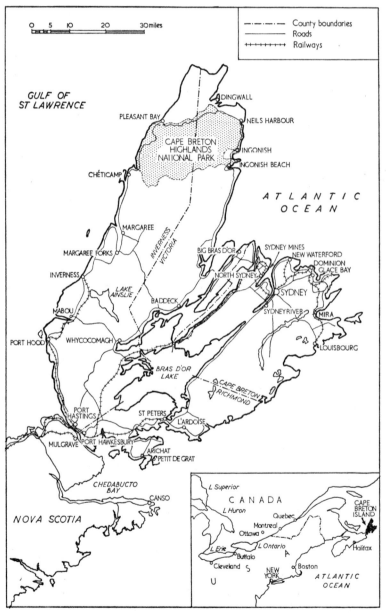

CAPE BRETON ISLAND

INTRODUCTION

Continents are much alike, and a man can no more love a continent than he can love a hundred million people. But all the islands of the world are different. They are small enough to be known, they are vulnerable, and men come to feel about them as they do about women.

Many men have loved the island of Cape Breton and a few may have hated her . . .

Hugh MacLennan

IT is easy to understand why this Canadian novelist and other native sons of Cape Breton Island have written about it with affection. For Cape Breton holds on to the hearts and minds of men with a strange tenacity. The land is hard, but lovely. Endless vistas of lake, hill and sky open up as the traveller crosses the island. No part of it, not even the untravelled interior of the northern plateau, is more than fifteen miles from water. Always the sea or the lakes are near, under an open sky and a wide horizon.

People came to Cape Breton Island, as they came to the rest of the New World, to seek resources or a better life. The quiet beauty and tranquillity of the land held many people even when economic conditions were not promising. It was the sea and the fish in it that first lured men to the coasts of Cape Breton.

The island did not appear as such until 1590, when Bartolomeu Lasso drew Cape Breton as a triangular body of land. Samuel de Champlain's map of 1632 showed a lake in the interior, and one settlement, Gransibou, which was probably on Sydney Harbour. He gave a thumbnail sketch that still holds as a good description of the island, 'Cape Breton is of a triangular form, eighty leagues in circuit, and is generally mountainous, nevertheless in some parts very pleasant . . .'

Cape Breton lies at the eastern end of Canada. Its northern peninsula looks like an admonishing finger held up by Canada to the island of Newfoundland, while the other fingers curl around the Bras d'Or Lake system in the centre of the island. Cape Breton was described in the Provincial Legislature as a 'tin can tied to a dog's tail' by one member, and as a 'jewel in a pig's snout' by another.

The island is 3,975 square miles in area, and is approximately 110 miles long by 87 miles wide. Its extreme southern tip, Cape Hogan on Isle Madame, lies at 45° 28' N; 61° 01' W. The northern promontory ends in two capes at the same latitude 47° 03' N: Cape St Lawrence on the west at 60° 36' W and Cape North on the east at 60° 25' W. The most easterly point is Cape Breton, at 45° 57' N; 59° 47' W. The point farthest west is Cape Linzee, about two miles north-west of Port Hood (46° 01' N; 61° 33' W).

The Cape Breton coastline stretches for 665 nautical miles. The Bras d'Or Lake system has a coastline of 443 nautical miles. This irregularly shaped lake system is 50 miles long by 20 miles wide, and covers about 450 square miles.

The island contains the most densely populated county in Nova Scotia (Cape Breton County—133 people to the square mile), the most sparsely populated (Victoria—seven people per square mile), and the smallest (Richmond). Inverness County, covering the western side of the island, is mainly farming, lumbering and fishing country. It has an area of 1,409 square miles and a population in 1971 of 20,375. The southern part was settled by Scots, the northern part by Acadians; the Margaree River mouth marks the contact point. Victoria County, with an area of 1,105 square miles, resembles a great wedge driven between Inverness County to the west, and Cape Breton to the east. Most of its 7,823 population live by fishing, farming, lumbering and tourism. Cape Breton County is rectangular shaped, with an area of 972 square miles. Its 129,075 population is mainly concentrated in a heavily urbanised belt in the northern part of the county where the coal mines and the steel mill are located. Fishing is another important activity. Richmond County in the south, with an area of 489 square miles and a population of 12,734, includes Isle Madame, where the people are predominantly Acadian in origin. In the past the county relied mainly on fishing. Now a new industrial complex has grown up at Point Tupper.

The names tell the story of the settlement of the island, and catch the flavour of the landscape. The lovely Indian name 'Whycocomagh' means 'head of the waters'. The Bras d'Or Lake system was probably named after Joao Fernandez, a Portuguese explorer who was a small squire or *llabrador*. The French names include 'Framboise' (raspberry) and 'L'Ardoise' (where there are slate cliffs). The Scottish names are everywhere, in Gaelic and English: Ben Eoin (Jonathan's Mountain), Craigmore (great rock), Dunvegan, Loch Lomond, Iona, Balmoral, Aberdeen and Inverness. Englishtown, where they did not have the Gaelic, was once *Bhal Na Ghul*, the town of the English. New Harris was once *Slois a Brochan*, the place of very thin gruel, but later Scottish settlers renamed it after their home. A man from Skye prospered at the head of the North-east Margaree, and felt he was king, so there is a settlement of Kingross there, just north of Portree. Other aspects of the island are revealed in the name Wreck Cove, and New Haven was once Hungry Cove.

Some soldiers who fought in the Peninsular War, and then in the War of 1812, settled on the shores of St Peter's Inlet and called their community 'Laugh at the Yankees'! It is now Soldier's Cove. People settled in small communities, usually with kin folk or friends.

Like most islanders, Cape Bretoners cherish their separate identity, yet seek closer links with the rest of Canada. Only 80ft of water now separates the two. This is the width of the lock in the canal that cuts through the eastern end of the Canso Causeway. When this causeway was completed on 10 December 1954, some Cape Bretoners claimed that 'no finger of land' was going to change their independent attitude. It is said that one old lady, leading the family prayers on the night the causeway was completed ended by saying, 'And, thank God for having at last made Canada a part of Cape Breton'!

The Strait of Canso which connects the Gulf of St Lawrence and the Atlantic Ocean is 14½ miles long and only 3,600ft wide at its narrowest point. At the landward end of the causeway stands Porcupine Hill, with half its face missing. From this hill, 10 million tons of rock were ripped and dumped into the strait, which has a maximum depth of 218ft here. The causeway, 4,300ft long, swings in a shallow *S* from mainland Nova Scotia at Auld's Cove to the island. The 8oft-wide causeway carries a 24ft highway section, a single-track railway line and a 6ft sidewalk.

The Canso Causeway created an ice-free port and has pushed Cape Breton into a new industrial era of oil refineries, pulp and paper mills, and heavy-water plants. But the essential rural quality of the island remains. Outside the Point Tupper-Port Hawkesbury and Sydney industrial areas, the land is lovely and almost untouched. The tree-clad hills rise from the sea, or from quiet river valleys like that of the Margaree. The tranquil atmosphere around the Bras d'Or Lakes seems to make time stand still. In the Cape Breton Highlands National Park in the northern finger of the island, the land is preserved for posterity. Here caribou and moose roam, the sea crashes on ancient rocks, and trails lead into deep valleys and up to the plateau rim where spectacular vistas of sea and mountain unfold under a clear, clean sky.

1 THE PHYSICAL ENVIRONMENT

THE island is made up of a series of uplands and lowlands. The uplands, underlain by pre-Cambrian crystalline rocks of great age, are made up of granites, syenites, quartzites, schists, gneisses, crystalline limestone and other metamorphic rocks. These are well exposed along the Cabot Trail, north of Petit Etang, in the Cape Breton Highlands National Park. The lowlands, which are on soft Carboniferous rocks, comprise conglomerates, shales, sandstone, gypsum, limestone and other sedimentary rocks. In summer, white limestone and gypsum outcrops gleam from the cliffs at Little Narrows, Plaster Cover, near Port Hawkesbury, and in the area around Cape North.

The bare bones of the island were formed more than 750 million years ago. At that time, during the pre-Cambrian era, volcanic rocks and sedimentary series were laid down. Through millions of years, these ancient rocks were folded, faulted, and changed by heat and pressure into gneisses and schists. They are black, dark green, grey, or even silvery looking; some contain small red garnet crystals.

During Devonian times, some 350 to 400 million years ago, these older rocks were intruded by great molten masses of igneous rock. This molten rock slowly cooled off, but narrow offshoots squeezed into the interstices of the older rocks, forming 'dykes'. At Green Cove, in Cape Breton Highlands National Park, granitic dykes criss-cross each other. After these intrusions, the rocks were again folded, faulted, broken and fractured into millions of individual blocks and pieces. The old hills of Cape

15

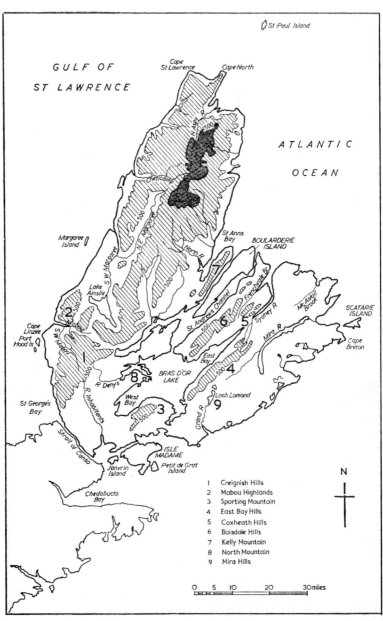

St Paul Island

GULF OF
ST LAWRENCE

Cape
St Lawrence   Cape North

ATLANTIC

OCEAN

Margaree
Island

St Anns
Bay   BOULARDERIE
ISLAND

Lake
Ainslie

SCATARIE
ISLAND

Cape
Linzee
Port
Hood Is

St Andrews Channel   Sydney R   Cape
Breton

East
Bay

BRAS D'OR
LAKE

St George's
Bay

West
Bay

Loch Lomond

Janvrin
Island

ISLE
MADAME
Petit de Grat
Island

Chedabucto
Bay

1   Creignish Hills
2   Mabou Highlands
3   Sporting Mountain
4   East Bay Hills
5   Coxheath Hills
6   Boisdale Hills
7   Kelly Mountain
8   North Mountain
9   Mira Hills

N

0   5   10   20   30 miles

CAPE BRETON ISLAND: PHYSICAL FEATURES

Breton stood in an ancient, forgotten sea, slowly eroded by winds, waves and weather. The rain washed the face of the land, the rivers cut down through the rocks, the waves nibbled at the edges of the newly created land, just as they are doing today. Sediments were deposited on top of the ancient rocks, and in the seas surrounding them. Erosion planed off the surface of the old land. During the Carboniferous era, about 280 million years ago, sandstones, conglomerates, shale, limestone, siltstones, and gypsum were formed, and the coal measures of Cape Breton were laid down in shallow, warm, primeval seas. The dazzling white gypsum deposits were formed when large areas of these ancient seas were cut off, and evaporation led to the precipitation of dissolved calcium sulphate. The limestones (calcium carbonate) which are mined at Irish Cove were also formed at this time. With the coal from the same era, the limestone formed the basis for the steelmaking industry that grew up in the Sydney area during the early part of this century.

Again, after the Carboniferous period, there was a time of uplift and erosion, with some faulting. In the northern part of the island, off the Cabot Trail, a wall of mountains appears beyond Dingwall. This wall is actually the face of the Aspy Fault which runs from north-east to south-west, and forms the North Aspy River Valley. What looks like a mountain range, as elsewhere on Cape Breton Island, is actually the edge of a plateau known as the old Atlantic Upland. Sugarloaf Mountain, on the road to Bay St Lawrence, is an isolated, cone-shaped outlier of this peneplane, the largest part of which forms the north pointing finger of Cape Breton Island. The elevations range from 1,200ft to about 1,500ft; White Hill, the highest point in Nova Scotia at 1,747ft, is located about 12 miles west of Ingonish. What appear to be isolated, scattered groups of hills—the Creignish Hills, the Boisdale Hills, Mabou Mountain, North Mountain, the East Bay Hills, the Mira Hills—are actually remnants of the old core rocks of the island. They have all been planed down so that their summits are roughly at the same height, and then tilted slightly from the north-west to the south-east. The South-eastern Upland between L'Ardoise and Scatarie stretches 10 to 15 miles inland, and slants beneath the sea in ragged peninsulas and islands. Here the rocky hills seldom exceed 200ft. The grain of the island runs south-west to north-east, at right angles to the direction of folding, as can be seen in the alignment of the Bras d'Or Lakes.

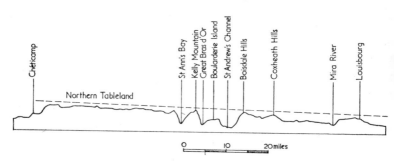

PROFILE ACROSS NORTHERN CAPE BRETON

In Cape Breton, the eye is constantly carried to the hills, all of which reach the same heights. Where the plateau reaches the sea, as along the northern parts of the Cabot Trail beyond Chéticamp and on the eastern side of the northern peninsula, the effect is spectacular. Cape Smoky drops sheer to the sea, its summit often shrouded in cloud, its feet washed by the waves. Usually there is a narrow band of carboniferous rocks between the crystalline rocks and the sea, along which runs the Cabot Trail.

Glaciation

Glaciation was the last major geological event to occur on Cape Breton Island before Man came to quarry the limestone and the gypsum and to rip the coal from underground seams. The glaciation of the island began a mere million years ago, and reached its peak about 40,000 years ago. During that time, there was a series of ice advances and retreats. Glaciologists are still working out the details of the ice movement, but the general trend of the ice advance, as over the rest of Acadia, was probably eastward, southward and south-westward. The weight of the ice sheet depressed the land, drowning the coast and flooding the interior of the island, and creating the Bras d'Or Lake system. St Andrew's Channel has depths down to 150 fathoms (approximately 914ft). Apparently, it was not ice action which deepened the Bras d'Or. One theory is that the great depths were created by the solution of underlying deposits of limestone and gypsum rocks.

The ice sheet covered the land, scraped off the soil and loose rock debris, polished rock surfaces, disturbed the drainage systems, gouged out lake basins and then retreated, leaving an irregular covering of boulders, sand and clay over the surface of the island. The glaciers rode out over the Scotian Shelf which lies to the east of Nova Scotia, leaving huge moraines there. A smaller number of moraines were deposited in south-east Cape Breton Island. Here, east of the Bras d'Or, the topography is a confused jumble of low ridges and winding rivers with thick forest all around. At Mary Anne Falls picnic area in the Cape Breton Highlands National Park, a small stream trickles over a smooth granite slope; the round boulders were transported to the spot by glaciers. At Warren Lake picnic ground, near Ingonish, the lake is a result of the partial damming of the valley of Warren Brook by glacial drift.

Around the coasts

The seas around Cape Breton work on the soft and hard rocks of the island. The early visitors could mine sea-coal out of the cliffs at places like Port Morien. But the coal measures, like the rest of the carboniferous rocks, are being eaten steadily away by coastal erosion. There have been reports of erosion at Cape Morien at a rate of 1½ft a year. Between 1907 and 1919, the northern side of Table Head, just beyond Glace Bay, had an accurately recorded average loss of 20ft per year. The coal seams exposed at Cape Morien in the early years of the eighteenth century had been washed away by 1920. In this area the average figure for erosion is 5–6in a year.

The sea taketh away, but the sea also giveth back. At places like Aspy Bay, South Bay, Ingonish and St Ann's Bay, the softer coastal rocks were submerged or worn away, but the sea has deposited long beaches at the entrances to the bays. At Aspy Bay, North Pond and South Pond there are *barachois*, fresh-water lakes cut off from the sea. At St Ann's Bay, however, the bar has not closed the entrance to the bay and a curving spit has formed, along which runs the road to the Englishtown ferry. The tide flowing in and out of the entrance to St Ann's Harbour keeps the narrow channel open. It is only 200ft wide where the depth is below 30ft, but it is another factor isolating northern Victoria County. All traffic travelling north of Smoky must either take this ferry or detour along the Cabot Trail, around the head of St Ann's Harbour.

The Bras d'Or Lakes are almost completely landlocked. To the south, the entrance is through St Peter's Canal. In the north-east there is a narrow, tortuous entrance to the lakes system through a passage to the east of Boularderie Island. This entrance is closed by breakers if a heavy sea is running. Great Bras d'Or, on the western side of Boularderie Island, is a mag-nificently straight and deep entrance. The straight sides of the channel are probably the result of faulting. Outside the Great Bras d'Or there are tidal ranges from 3 to 5ft. Inside the lakes the range is only 1½ft, and the spring tides at Baddeck rise only 6in. This makes the lakes ideal for yachting, though small waves, up to 1ft in height, can disturb the placid surface of the lake when a sudden gust of wind blows.

A number of small islands lie off the coast of Cape Breton. St Paul Island lies about 13 miles off the tip of the island. Its northern point is a detached rock, separated by a very narrow channel from a peninsula 408ft high. An isthmus joins this peninsula to the main body of the island, which comprises two parallel ranges of hills. The whole island is very inaccessible and surrounded by deep water. Scatarie Island, which lies off the south-eastern coast of Cape Breton County, has a different aspect, although it has been equally hazardous to ships. Its coast has low cliffs and a crenalate shoreline, its highest point rising to 191ft.

Two islands lie off Port Hood. The smallest, to the south, is Henry Island. The larger, Port Hood Island, is settled and farmed. At one time, it was linked by a sandspit to the mainland, but this was nibbled away by the sea in the nineteenth century. Chéticamp Island is linked to the mainland by a spit on the south side which turns an open roadstead into a reasonable harbour. Margaree Island, also known as Sea Wolf Island, is of sandstone, surrounded by submerged rocks and strong tides.

The north-west coast of Cape Breton is a bold one; between Cape St Lawrence and Cape Linzee there is only one harbour, at Chéticamp. Elsewhere landings can only be made at the mouths of ravines and small streams. The south-east coast, from Bear Head at the entrance to the Strait of Canso to Scatarie Island, is a tattered, ragged edge of land. Isle Madame, a low, flat area, is an integral part of Cape Breton. From Point Michaud to Gabarus Bay, the coast is low lying, barren and rocky. There are numerous lakes and ponds, and some reddish clay cliffs that reach heights of from 70 to 90ft. In fog, this is an eerie coast, but in sunshine the great waves are a splendid sight as they ride in over beautiful sandy beaches at places like Point Michaud.

The best harbours are around the coasts of Cape Breton County. Louisbourg has a good one, and Sydney Harbour is an inlet with an entrance $2\frac{1}{2}$ miles wide. The inlet runs southward for about 5 miles, dividing at Point Edward into North-west Arm and South Arm. Sydney Harbour is on South Arm.

CAPE BRETON ISLAND

Rivers

   The surface of Cape Breton Island is drained by a large number of short streams. Sydney River rises near the head of East Bay, then straggles along through a series of lakes until it flows into the South Arm at the small community named after it. The northern plateau is deeply dissected by short streams that flow in deep gorges. From the east end of the Chéticamp camping ground, the Salmon Pool Trail leads up a typical river valley, whose spurs interlock. The Chéticamp River hurries rapidly to the Gulf of St Lawrence, crossing a narrow coastal plain after it emerges from the edge of the plateau. On the western side of the island, the main rivers are the Chéticamp, Grand Anse, Margaree, Mabou and Mull, which drain into the Gulf of St Lawrence or Northumberland Strait. The east and south sides of the island are drained by the North Aspy, Ingonish, Indian, Barachois, North, Mira, Catalone, Framboise, Grand, Tillard and Inhabitants Rivers, which flow into the Atlantic Ocean. The Mira River, rising behind Gabarus Bay, curves around the barren area behind Louisbourg to flow into Mira Bay through Mira Gut. It is a wide pleasant river whose shores are dotted with summer cottages. The road from Sydney to Louisbourg crosses it at Albert Bridge, a mile or two south of which the coastal fog belt begins. The Baddeck, Skye, Black, Washabuck and Middle Rivers drain into the Bras d'Or Lakes. After the Cabot Trail leaves the shores of the Bras d'Or west of Baddeck, it follows the Middle River valley. The Mira and the Margaree were once vital lines of communication into the interior, and are now suitable for canoeing.

   On the lowland plains, where gypsum and limestone occur, sinkholes have been formed by the collapse of the surface, following solution of the rocks. In 1952, two farm horses were swallowed in the mud near Lakes O'Law when the roof of a cave collapsed. There are a number of caves in the Cape

22

Dauphin area, formed by solution. Here the gypsum deposits are up to 200ft in thickness.

Soils

There are no first-class soils on Cape Breton Island. This harsh fact became apparent to settlers who sought to cultivate a land whose natural cover was cool, temperate forest. Soil-forming processes have been at work since the ice sheet melted, some 10,000 years ago. The results of a soil survey, reported in 1963, noted that soils developed from glacial till occupied about 56 per cent of the island. Of these, about 60 per cent were well drained, 30 per cent imperfectly drained, and the rest poorly drained. Soils formed from glacio-fluvial parent material covered about 3·5 per cent of the island. The remaining 40 per cent of the soils consisted of peat, salt marsh, and rough mountain land.

The soils need careful management, with particular attention to drainage, fertilisation, liming, and stone removal. The early settlers knew nothing of the chemical composition or suitability for agriculture of the island soils, which were covered by thick forest to the water's edge. Many areas cleared for agriculture have now reverted to forest; this process can be seen going on all over the island at the present time. In five years, spruce and pine can get a firm grip on land that was once used for crops or pasture.

Most of the cultivated soils were developed on fine-textured parent materials; they occupy 16·5 per cent of the surveyed area. Soils developed on moderately coarse textured parent materials occupy 38 per cent of the island, and only 10 per cent of the area occupied by these soils is suitable for agriculture. On one series of these soils (the Thom Series), on top of Mabou Mountain, a community pasture has been established. Also, in the Mabou area a number of Dutch farmers are successfully farming poor soils. Some soils have not been broken for agriculture. About 2–3 per cent of the island, some 62,658 acres, is covered with peat soils. About 45 per cent of these soils occur on high elevations on upland plateau areas in Inverness and Victoria Counties. In Cape Breton Highland National Park, on the upland area south of Pleasant Bay there is an exhibit on High Bogs, and a walkway is laid out over a patch of bog. The peat soils are covered with scattered stands of tamarack, black spruce and red maple, but most of the ground cover is sphagnum moss, labrador tea, lambkill, ground juniper, bog rosemary, cottongrass and crowberry. Rough mountain land covers 34 per cent of the surface area of the island, or some 919,675 acres. Most of this is in northern Inverness and Victoria Counties, and these soils carry good tree growth—balsam fir, red spruce, white spruce, wire birch, grey birch, beech, black spruce, tamarack and some pine. Salt marshes cover 876 acres, coastal beaches 4,654 acres and mining dumps 988 acres.

SOIL CAPABILITY

Class	Characteristics	Best use	Acreage
II	Good crop land, moderate limitations	Agriculture	47,960
III	Good to fair crop land—moderately severe limitations	Agriculture—restricted choice of crops	495,753
IV	Fair to poor crop land—severe limitations	Hay—pasture	126,384
V	Very wet soils	Grazing—forestry	43,126
VI	Very stony, steep or shallow	Forestry—limited grazing	764,095
VII	Rock outcrops, very stony or steep slopes	Forestry and wildlife	1,019,523

CLIMATE AND WEATHER

A Cape Breton writer has summarised the weather as 'a wonderful summer and fall climate, a hard winter and a rotten spring'. In midsummer, puffy cumulus clouds hang in a blue sky and the heat haze blurs the outlines of the low hills that seem to line

every horizon. The smell of balsam hangs on the air when the
truckloads of pulpwood pass by. In the fall, the air is clear, and
endless vistas of changing autumn colours show up clearly. In
the winter, the land is black and white under a steel-grey sky
and rain often splashes across the landscape.

The key feature of the climate is its changeability: on 10–11
May 1972, 11·1in of snow fell at Sydney Airport; on 29 May,
the station recorded a high of 87° F. Cape Breton Island lies
in the lee of North America so that its climate is a result of
continental as well as oceanic forces. Two large atmospheric
systems dominate the weather over most of the Maritime
Provinces: the Icelandic Low, between Greenland and Iceland,
with its anticlockwise winds, and the Bermuda-Azores High,
with clockwise winds. The Icelandic Low brings strong north-
westerly winds in winter; the Bermuda-Azores High brings
summer westerlies. From the south come hurricanes which
sometimes reach the Maritimes in summer and fall as severe
gales. Indeed, Cape Breton is located at the point in North
America where most storm systems head out into the Atlantic;
they give a dying kick before they disappear into the east.
Throughout the winter, there is a steady stream of storms down
the St Lawrence Valley that often head out to sea along the
Gulf of St Lawrence and batter the island's north-west coast.
Other storms sometimes travel up the east coast of the United
States and affect the east coast of Cape Breton Island, bringing
pockets of warm maritime air into the area, which turns the
snow into rain and wipes the land clear. In spring and early
summer, cold continental air sometimes descends across the
island, dropping temperatures and bringing night frosts. Ice
surrounds the western and northern coasts from January to
early May. This ice forms in winter and breaks up in the spring
when the ice in the Gulf of St Lawrence begins to move and to
pack against the island's west coast. The southern coast, facing
the open Atlantic, has only a light and scattered ice cover in the
winter; the area around Isle Madame and the entrance to the

25

Strait of Canso has open water all year round. Nowadays, planes fly regular ice patrols over the Gulf of St Lawrence; icebreakers are stationed at Sydney to keep the port open all through the year, and there is a central recording office on ice conditions at Sydney.

The perils of travel on these seas before such modern aids to ice navigation are amply documented in *Ensign Prenties's Narrative*. In November 1780 Ensign Prenties, a somewhat individualistic young man, full of grievances, and with a dislike for the restraints of military life, was on his way from Quebec to New York in the brigantine *St Lawrence*. The ship leaked and the captain drank. A north-west wind drove them on shore in a snowstorm, and the ship grounded near the mouth of Margaree Harbour. Here the snow was waist deep. A boy fell into the sea, was rescued, fell asleep on the shore, and froze to death. Three other survivors died of frostbite and exposure—and this was in early December! Ensign Prenties set out in a small boat and travelled 140 miles up the coast, noting 'prodigious quantities of ice' on the coast. North of Chéticamp, the sea froze in a gale, and then cleared in a south-east gale off the land. It rained and snowed, and game was scarce; finally the party was rescued by Indians and taken to St Peter's.

January is the snowiest month. The area north-west of the Bras d'Or Lakes gets a heavier snowfall than the area to the south-west. Observers report seeing snow falling near Whycocomagh on the TransCanada Highway while around St Peter's, on highway 4, there was no snow at all and skies were clear. And heavy winter snow is a constant problem to highway operations in the Middle River area. All the stations are located at low elevations, and most are on or near the coast, so, if anything, they give a somewhat milder and wetter picture of the climate than prevails in the inland areas. Rainfall amounts also vary considerably.

The graphs for the Sydney Airport probably give the best picture of the temperature regime on Cape Breton Island.

Place	Location	Height a s l	Yrs of record	Mean daily temp (°F)	Record max temp (°F)	Record min temp (°F)	Days with frost	Total precip (inches)	Snowfall (inches)	Rainfall (inches)
Port Hastings	45° 38' N 61° 23' W	75ft	31–35	43·2	99	−16	158	47·46	64·8	41·02
Port Hood	46° 01' N 61° 34' W	25ft	10–12	42·5	90	−11	161	52·37	82·5	44·56
Chéticamp	46° 39' N 60° 57' W	0ft	10–12	42·8	88	−15	157	51·79	176·4	34·13
St Paul Island	47° 12' N 60° 09' W	104ft	27–8	40·9	86	−10	163	35·36	88·8	26·44
Ingonish Beach	46° 39' N 60° 24' W	15ft	20–1	43·4	94	−14	159	64·70	135·4	51·19
Sydney Airport	46° 10' N 60° 03' W	197ft	29–30	42·8	95	−13	162	52·78	113·4	41·47
Margaree Forks	46° 22' N 61° 05' W	50ft	10–11	41·8	90	−24	175	50·45	143·0	36·15
Baddeck	46° 06' N 60° 45' W	25ft	39–43	43·3	98	−26	156	49·00	89·7	40·06
Loch Lomond	45° 44' N 60° 37' W	100ft	7–13	NA	NA	NA	NA	53·74	63·1	46·64

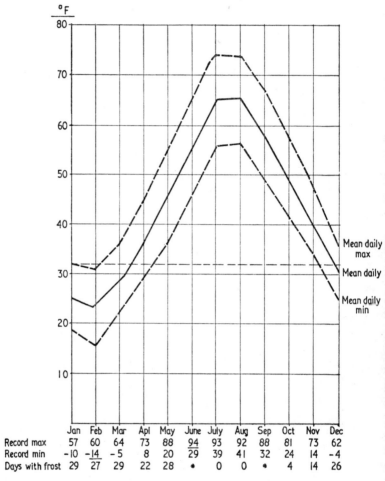

	Jan	Feb	Mar	Apl	May	June	July	Aug	Sep	Oct	Nov	Dec
Record max	57	60	64	73	88	94	93	92	88	81	73	62
Record min	-10	-14	-5	8	20	29	39	41	32	24	14	-4
Days with frost	29	27	29	22	28	*	0	0	*	4	14	26

TEMPERATURE REGIME: SYDNEY AIRPORT

Temperatures reach the minimum in February, then there is a slow rise through the spring to the maxima in July–August, when the temperature curve flattens out. Spring tends to linger long, and the arrival of summer is delayed by the pack ice around the coast, and the frequent north-east winds. There is a slow and gentle slide into fall, which is the golden season on the island with warm days and cool nights. DEVCO (The Cape Breton Development Corporation), seeking to boost tourism as an aid to the development of the island, are pressing for an extension of the season into September and October. However, even they are reticent about the weather from April through to early June.

July is the sunniest month, recording more than 250 hours of sunshine. The summer heat is usually softened with a breeze. November, December and January have fewer than 100 hours of sunshine in each month, and the winter winds make that season chillier. The northern plateau region, a subarctic barren, has long cold winters and short cool summers. Here the snow lies deep in sheltered places in July, and the vegetation crouches near the ground to gain some protection from the winds.

The violence of the winds and sudden changes in the weather have brought perils to the life of the islanders. Each fishing village has a long list of men lost at sea. On the other hand, ships that sank or were driven ashore often provided a rich haul for beachcombers. At Chéticamp, the local historian recorded that 1874 was known as 'L'année de la farine', because of the flour that floated ashore in that year. Several years later, there was the 'butter summer' when a thousand pounds of butter in small tins was cast up on the shore. And best of all was 'L'année du rhum', a gala day, 25 October 1931, when a jettisoned cargo of rum from a smugglers' boat came ashore near Chéticamp. On this coast blows the terrible *suêtes*, a local wind from the south-east. It descends from the interior of the plateau during the summer, and everyone in Chéticamp stays at home. Summer gales are also common elsewhere on the island.

On 24 August 1873, a severe storm struck Cape Breton Island. Many ships disappeared in the open sea, and it was said that a thousand Nova Scotia seamen never returned home. At Port

Morien, thirty-seven vessels were driven ashore. Roofs were torn off in Sydney and North Sydney; two hundred buildings were blown down on Isle Madame. Torrential rain accompanied the storm, and six bridges were carried away. This 'August Gale' (originally known as the Lord's Day Gale) was probably the tail end of a tropical hurricane; a similar storm raced across eastern Nova Scotia in August 1971. In March 1947, while the Nova Scotia Power Commission was still struggling with the problems of getting electricity to people on Cape Breton, the system's Cansean network was almost completely destroyed by sleet and ice, driven by an 80mph gale which broke the transmission lines and left wires and towers strewn across the countryside. The line was rebuilt in ten days, but a second storm of equal intensity ripped through the same section.

VEGETATION

With a cool and somewhat damp climate, the natural cover of Cape Breton Island is Acadian forest. There are about 2,700 square miles of productive forest land on the island. About 65 per cent of this is softwood, and about 6 per cent hardwood; the remainder is made up of mixed softwood-hardwood stands. Conifers cover the lowland areas, and much of the upland plateau. The commonest trees are white and red spruce and balsam fir. The maple, yellow birch, wire birch, poplar, ash, beech and alder are the main deciduous trees and occupy many of the mountainous slopes. These slopes, which appear to be bald or covered in dead trees in the winter and spring, burst into brilliant greens in the summer, dying out in the fall in a blaze of orange, red and brown.

On upland areas, where drainage is poor, there is sparse, stunted vegetation, mainly black spruce and tamarack. Peat bog occupies the wet areas; the areas of sphagnum moss are surrounded by black spruce, tamarack and alder. In industrial Cape Breton, the conifers and other hardwoods are affected by

30

industrial fumes, and dense forest is absent from the roadside. Some scrub poplar and wire birch struggle to exist, and there is thick ground-cover of labrador tea, huckleberry, blueberry and numerous small shrubs.

The early settlers cleared the land indiscriminately, using the largest timbers for house and boat building. In Inverness and Victoria Counties especially, much land is going back to forest. The trees circle the clearings, seemingly waiting for the farmers to leave. The spruce trees seed into the cleared fields, and grow rapidly. Small spruce trees are unpalatable to live-stock, and so survive even in heavily grazed areas. Fir and hardwood seedlings are grazed off, but where there is little or no grazing of cleared areas, the balsam fir becomes the dominant new growth.

At the same time, the forest areas are periodically ravaged by fire. Cape Smoky went up in flames in June 1962. The fire, started by carelessness, could be seen at Sydney, over thirty miles away, and it burned 4,200 acres. In 1947, on the other side of the northern plateau, fire burned 7,000 acres of hard-woods in the Grand Anse Valley and Highland Coniferous Forest. The fire burned for fifteen days and partially destroyed the village of Pleasant Bay. The burnt-over areas reseed naturally. First comes the aptly-named fireweed, followed by biennials and perennials such as bristly aralia, blueberries and raspberries. Then come aspens, wild cherries and birches; these are mostly weed trees, which provide cover for the seed-lings of spruce and fir. In time, these conifers form a new forest, replacing the one that was burnt over.

Most of the wild flowers that spring and summer bring to Cape Breton can be found along or near the roadsides. Some, like the oxeye daisy, are not native to the island but were introduced from Europe. The French call this flower the marguerite, and one tradition is that the Margaree Valley, where it abounds, was named after it. Another flower growing wild and in colour-ful profusion along the highway is the lupin. Angelica, once

31

cultivated by the eighteenth-century inhabitants of Louisbourg for medicinal purposes, now grows wild. The tiny strawberries which can be picked in substantial quantities in roadside fields make delicious eating, as do the wild raspberries which ripen a little later. Less accessible are the blueberries which grow in the barrens. The bake-apple, found in boggy areas of Cape Breton, parts of mainland Nova Scotia and Newfoundland, bears no resemblance to an apple. It is like a raspberry in form and texture, but golden in colour.

WILD LIFE

Most species of wild life on the mainland of Nova Scotia— black bears, beaver, bobcat, chipmunk, otter and snowshoe hares—are represented on Cape Breton Island, with the exception of the skunk and the porcupine. Richard Uniacke, writing in the 1860s, described how the Indians, who used the long porcupine quills for ornamental craftwork, had often tried to introduce the animal to the island, but it never survived for long. The racoon, easily recognised by its black-ringed eyes, grey-ringed tail and strong penchant for raiding garbage cans, has recently become established in isolated areas; it is believed to have been brought in from Maine, and released illegally.

A relative newcomer to the island is the white-tailed deer, so-called from the white underside of its tail, which it raises like a flag as it bounds away. Introduced into Cape Breton in the early 1920s, it is now the most important big-game species. A handsome creature, it can sometimes be seen from the road in the Margaree Valley, among other places, especially where field and forest meet. Its coat is reddish-brown in summer, grey and heavier in winter. The male has distinctive antlers; one to five spikes project, more or less forward from one main beam.

Two animals once plentiful on Cape Breton have recently been re-introduced: the moose, which was hunted to extinction by the beginning of this century, and the caribou, which had

Page 33 (above) Cap Rouge on the north-western coast of Breton Island, looking south; (below) Cap Rouge in winter, looking north. The road is part of the Cabot Trail

Page 34 (*above*) The settlement of Chéticamp stretches along the Cabot Trail. In the background is part of Cape Breton Highlands National Park; (*left*) white-tailed deer can sometimes be seen from the road in Cape Breton. This one, however, was photographed in a mainland game park

died out by the early 1920s. The animals were established in Cape Breton Highlands National Park. Eighteen moose from the Elk Island National Park in Alberta were brought to Cape Breton in 1947. In 1968 eighteen woodland caribou were transferred into the park from the Laurentides Provincial Park in Quebec, and thirty-two others were added in 1969.

The lynx, though very rare in mainland Nova Scotia, still inhabits remote wooded parts of Cape Breton. A handsome, stub-tailed cat with thick soft fur, it can be distinguished from its relative, the bobcat, by its longer legs and ear tufts; its higher hindquarters give it an odd 'downhill' gait.

The marten, a weasel-like mammal whose lustrous fur was once eagerly sought by trappers, is now a protected species and thrives on Cape Breton Island, though it is extinct in mainland Nova Scotia. Its best known relative is the Russian sable of Europe and Asia.

There are several species of salamander on the island, and six species of frog. In spring and early summer, the shrill chorus of the spring peepers can be heard almost everywhere. Pickerel, wood and leopard frogs are found in a variety of habitats, and the green frog, with its call like the plucking of an untuned banjo, is more often heard than seen.

The snakes are non-poisonous. The commonest is the garter snake, a gregarious creature that gathers in large numbers to hibernate in the fall. The redbellied, ringnecked and green snake are also found.

Birds

Cape Breton plays host to a wide variety of birds, both residents and visitors stopping off in the course of their migrations. More than 170 species have been observed in and around the Cape Breton Highlands National Park. A distinguished resident is the bald eagle, the official symbol of the USA where it is yearly growing rarer. The eagle is not, in fact, bald; it has a head of white feathers, which together with the white tail

c

feathers give the bird its distinctive appearance. It nests in the National Park and in uninhabited areas around the shores of Bras d'Or. It is legally protected, and seems to know it, sitting serene, aloof and solitary at the top of a tree, or travelling down the flyways of the river valleys. The red-tailed hawk, the goshawk and the barred owl are other resident birds of prey. A rarer sight is the osprey, easily identifiable by its habit of diving for fish feet first, then emerging from the water with its prey clutched between its claws.

The chief game-birds are ruffed grouse and Hungarian partridge. On Scatarie Island, an experiment is under way to introduce another species of game-bird, the willow ptarmigan. Sixty were brought from Newfoundland and released on Scatarie in 1969. They appear to be not only surviving, but increasing in numbers. The Provincial Wildlife Department's hope is that the birds will become abundant enough to make their way to the Cape Breton mainland. If the venture is a success, it is planned to repeat the experiment with sharp-tailed grouse.

Many songbirds brighten the Cape Breton landscape in spring and summer; the blue jay with its harsh call and bright blue plumage; the redstart fanning out its tail into flashes of orange; the bright yellow goldfinch and the black-capped chickadee are only a few that add colour and sound to wood and meadow. The robin is seen in town and country; unlike the English robin, it is actually a species of thrush with a brick-red breast. Early settlers to North America, homesick for England, gave the bird its name, and it is every bit as self-assured and impudent as its European namesake.

The migrating birds stopping over on Cape Breton include several species of duck. The ring-necked duck, common golden-eye and mergansers are among those that breed on the island. One group of ducks has adjusted to urban living and resides all the year round in Wentworth Park in downtown Sydney. Herring gulls and black-backed gulls hover over town rubbish dumps and follow the inland farmer's plough as well as soaring over the sea-coast. Gannets, terns, great cormorants and puffins swell the seabird population, and all these species can be seen on the Bird Islands (Ciboux Island and Hertford Island) that lie off Cape Dauphin, near the entrance to Great Bras d'Or. The long coastline of the Bras d'Or Lake system is the haunt of a number of waterbirds, including the great blue heron and double-crested cormorant.

Fish

The Margaree is famous for its Atlantic salmon; one caught at Big Intervale in 1927 weighed 52½lb. This highly prized game fish is also taken from the Chéticamp and Grand Rivers, although in all three rivers the supply has been declining. Unlike the Pacific salmon, the Atlantic salmon does not die after spawning, but returns to the sea. At this stage the fish is thin and its distinctive deep blue back and silvery sides have become dark. It is known then as a kelt or slink, and in Nova Scotia the catching or even possession of a slink is illegal. At North-east Margaree, a former schoolhouse has been turned into a salmon museum, with exhibits relating to the salmon's life cycle, its pursuit by man, and the equipment used, both legal and illegal.

Another fish popular with sports fishermen is the eastern brook trout which is found in many Cape Breton rivers, including the Margaree. Brown trout, introduced into Nova Scotia waters in 1933, flourish in Kilkenny Lake, about five miles north of Sydney. Lakes and streams in the National Park are regularly stocked with trout. In the spring, alewives, known locally as gaspereaux, come up the Margaree in great numbers to spawn. They are caught chiefly for bait. In the winter, eels and smelts are caught through the ice; the eel fishery was especially important to the early Indians.

One of the most challenging of the salt-water game fish is the bluefin tuna. Cape Breton holds the world record for the largest ever taken by an angler. It weighed 1,065lb and was

37

landed in St George's Bay, near Port Hawkesbury, on 19 November 1970. Another fighting game fish in Cape Breton waters is the swordfish.

Harbour seals are found along the coast from Louisbourg to Chedabucto Bay, and there is a breeding colony of grey seals on Point Michaud, on the south coast. In the Bras d'Or Lake system, grey seals have been found in the woods over two miles from shore. They feed on the cod and mackerel in the lakes, and are common around Washabuck, swimming up the Denys River in the spring. While the grey and harbour seals may delight the visitor, they are a nuisance to fishermen. They interfere with fishing nets, and are carriers of cod-worm, that affects the flesh of cod, plaice and other fish. In late March or early April, young harp seals may be seen in the open sea off western and northern Cape Breton.

2   HISTORY

RCHAEOLOGICAL evidence for a prehistory of Cape
Breton Island is very scanty, and only two sites occupied
by succeeding Indian cultures have been excavated, one
at North Aspy and one at Little Narrows. The site at Little
Narrows, excavated by J. S. Erskine of the Nova Scotia Museum,
yielded artifacts covering approximately three thousand years.

The Micmac Indians of Cape Breton were nomadic hunters
and gatherers before the Europeans arrived. During the winter
they hunted moose, caribou and other woodland game.
Equipped with snowshoes, the Indians found it easy to hunt
the moose in thick snow. With the killing of his first moose, a
boy became a man. In summer, the Micmacs moved to the
shore where they lived on fish, shellfish, and berries gathered
by the women. Their method of catching lobsters at night
yielded large numbers. The lobster, always curious, were lured
to the shore by the light from burning torches, and then speared
in the shallows. The Micmac shelter was a conical wigwam,
constructed from four spruce poles covered with birch bark.
The entrance always faced the rising sun. Birch bark was also
used for making canoes. The social organisation of the Micmac
was based on a clan unit. Each unit had its own symbol. These
symbols, which included a cross, were tattooed on the skin and
painted or embroidered in porcupine quills on clothing and
other personal possessions.

CAPE BRETON ISLAND

EUROPEAN DISCOVERY AND EXPLORATION

The first European visitors to the coast of Cape Breton Island may have been Norsemen sailing south from Vinland, which was probably sited in northern Newfoundland. Basque and Breton fishermen, too, according to tradition, were plying these waters before Columbus crossed the Atlantic.

The most controversial aspect of the area's early history is the exact location of John Cabot's landfall. Cabot, who had made trading voyages to the East, was interested in finding a western route to Asia. In 1496, he received patents from Henry VII which allowed him, 'full and free authority, leave, and power to sail . . . to all parts, countreys, and seas of the East, of the West, and of the North, under our banners and ensignes, with five ships'. Cabot succeeded in fitting out only ship, the *Mathew*, in which he set sail from Bristol in May 1497. On 24 June he reached land, went ashore and planted a cross. From contemporary letters and a map, the landfall has been placed at a variety of locations: near what is now Portland, Maine; Cape Bonavista, Newfoundland; Cape St Lewis, Labrador; Cape Bauld and Cape Dégrat, Newfoundland—and Cape Breton Island. In the northern part of Victoria County, a cairn, surmounted by a bust of John Cabot, has been erected by the Cape Breton Historical Society. The inscription reads

ON 24TH JUNE 1497 IN THE 'MATHEW' OUT OF BRISTOL, ENGLAND, WITH A CREW OF EIGHTEEN MEN, JOHN CABOT DISCOVERED THE CONTINENT OF NORTH AMERICA. HIS LAND-FALL 'FIRST LAND SEEN' WAS IN THIS VICINITY AND IS BELIEVED TO HAVE BEEN THE LOFTY HEADLAND OF NORTH CAPE BRETON.

When Cabot returned from his voyage he brought news of a vast abundance of fish and, in the following century, fishermen of a dozen nations flocked to the area. At first, the only method

40

of preserving the fish was to salt them in brine. The Mediter-
ranean countries were well supplied with solar salt, but the
Norman, Breton and English fishermen early on switched from
'wet' or 'green' fishing to drying fish. For this they had to come
ashore and erect 'flakes' or drying stages. This method of
preservation resulted in a better price for the fish; soon all the
fishermen were using it and Cape Breton became an international haven. The French used St Ann's Bay; the English
preferred English Harbour (later Louisbourg), and the
Spaniards Spanish Bay, later known as Sydney Harbour.

During this time, a Portuguese, Joao Alvares Fagundes, who
had made a voyage around the Cape Breton coast, applied to
the king of Portugal for rights to the whole island. Sometime
around 1525, he established a settlement at Ingonish, which
lasted about a year. Supplies from the homeland were not
forthcoming and the local Indians became hostile when they
realised the white men intended to settle.

At the beginning of the seventeenth century, no European
power had a clear claim to what are now the Maritime Provinces of Canada. The French established New France, which
included 'Canada' (the land along the St Lawrence) and
'Acadia' (the present Maritime Provinces). Their hold on the
area was tenuous, however, and for a hundred years there were
raids, counter-raids, and disputes in Acadia not only between
English and French but between different groups of Frenchmen
who claimed exclusive rights over certain areas.

In 1621 Sir William Alexander, a Scot, decided that he would
like to own Acadia. He received a charter for the territory under
the name of New Scotland, or Nova Scotia, as it was written in
Latin. Shortly after, rights to Prince Edward Island and Cape
Breton Island were transferred to Sir Robert Gordon of Lochin-
var. To encourage settlement, baronetcies were sold. To make
sure that the new baronets of Nova Scotia were created in the
proper feudal manner, a small section of Edinburgh Castle was
designated Nova Scotia. It remains so to this day.

41

In 1629 James Stewart, Lord Ochiltree, having bought a baronetcy for 200 livres sterling, equipped a ship and sailed with sixty immigrants to Cape Breton to set up a colony. He landed in the harbour of Baleine, got down to clearing the land and then sent out a boat to collect tribute from the foreign fishermen in the area. This was a mistake. The fishermen complained to Captain Charles Daniel, an employee of the Company of New France. On his way to Quebec, Daniel had been blown off-course into St Ann's Bay where he had begun to build a fort. He captured Ochiltree and his settlers and took them to St Ann's. There he set them to work on his fort and, with their help, also built a house, chapel and magazine. Lord Ochiltree was later taken to France and tried unsuccessfully to get compensation. The rest of the prisoners were returned to England. When Daniel sailed with them, he left behind a garrison of fifty men, more than a third of whom had died of scurvy by the time he returned.

The next attempt at settlement was made by Nicholas Denys, who came out to Acadia in 1632 with Governor de Razilly. On the governor's death, two men, Charles de La Tour and Charles de Menou d'Aulnay, fought for control of Acadia. After being ousted from his post at Port Rossignol and later from Miscou by d'Aulnay, Denys moved to Cape Breton where he established posts at St Peter's and St Ann's. Once more he was turned out, this time by d'Aulnay's widow, who had become Madame La Tour. Re-established at St Peter's, Denys was dispossessed this time by one of d'Aulnay's creditors, Le Borgne, who took him prisoner to Port Royal. When the English under Robert Sedgewick captured Port Royal in 1654, he was released and went back to France. From the king, Denys obtained letters patent confirming his control over Cape Breton and other areas. The fort at St Peter's was surrendered by Le Borgne, and for the first time Denys was able to live serenely, with his wife and children, in his own domain. In 1668, he was burned out of St Peter's and moved to the mainland. Shortly afterwards, he returned to France, where he published *Description Géo-graphique et historique des costes de l'Amerique septentrionale, avec l'histoire naturelle du pais.* This book, which appeared in 1672, contains the first authentic description of Cape Breton Island.

THE FRENCH RÉGIME

In 1713, Cape Breton Island became the key to the retention of Canada by France. Under the terms of the Treaty of Utrecht, France was forced to give up Acadia and Newfoundland, and was left with only the Ile St Jean (Prince Edward Island) and Ile Royale (Cape Breton Island). Despite Britain's opposition, a clause in the treaty gave France the right to fortify Ile Royale.

The French brought a group of 180 settlers, mainly fishermen and their families from Placentia in Newfoundland, as the first step towards populating the island. They were accompanied by the Governor, de Costebelle, who complained that he was exchanging one sterile desert for another. The settlers were landed at English Harbour. They had a miserable winter, losing all their horses and having to slaughter all but two of their cattle.

English Harbour, renamed Louisbourg in honour of the reigning French monarch, was eventually chosen as the location of a fortress. Designed by Verville and Verrier in the tradition of Vauban, the builder of France's greatest fortresses, the six bastions connected by curtain walls gave Louisbourg its characteristic star-shape. The King's Bastion, with the Château St Louis, comprised the Citadel. The château contained the governor's apartments, chapel, officers' quarters, barracks and store rooms. The land side of the fortress was protected by massive earthworks, glacis and an 8oft-wide ditch. The harbour was guarded by the guns of the Royal Battery on the shore facing the entrance, and by the guns of the Island Battery at the entrance itself.

The mightiest fortress in North America, Louisbourg was an impressive sight and it was meant to be. It was the key to the defence of Canada. The masonry-faced walls were 12ft thick, but the mortar of lime and saltwater began to crumble after the first frost. Caen stone was imported from France for the cut-stone work, but most of this was used for the Governor's apartments, or sold to the New Englanders. For although *les Bostonnais* might gaze in awed apprehension at the huge edifice, it did not stop them trading with the French. In one year they sold fourteen boatloads of timber and one thousand barrels of flour to Louisbourg. Inside the walls, there was a large hospital, taverns, an ice-house, shops, and houses, many of them built of stone. There was nothing like it to be found in the English colonies.

But all was not well with the fortifications. Although there were embrasures for 148 guns, only seventy-nine had been supplied. Louis XV was having enough trouble finding artillery for his continental wars, and could spare no more guns or money for Louisbourg. The fortress, which had cost the enormous sum of 30 million livres, was manned by Swiss mercenaries, an unsatisfactory and expensive body of men.

Another weakness was the failure of the fortress to become self-sufficient. Despite the glowing promises made to them by the French, the wholesale migration of Acadian farmers from British Nova Scotia to Ile Royale did not materialise. The settlers who did come were mainly fishermen, and not interested in agriculture. The inhabitants of Louisbourg were obliged to rely on shipments of food from France and purchases from Nova Scotia, Canada and New England. Due partly to the appalling improvidence of Governor Du Quesnel, Louisbourg was short of food at the end of the winter of 1743–4, and the residents were only saved from starvation by the last-minute arrival of provisions from Quebec.

Even with abundant food, this isolated, cold and fog-bound area would depress the average soldier. Cramped quarters, corrupt officers, tattered uniforms, no boots, and pay six months in arrears added to his discontent. Mutiny finally broke out in December 1744. The mutineers took over the town, and forced

44

the Governor and the Intendant to give them their back pay
and some decent food. Through the whole winter and into the
spring, Louisbourg was in a state of anarchy.

In May 1744, war had broken out between Britain and France.
Du Quesnel attempted to boost his sagging reputation by
attacking Canso, a British fishing post on the mainland opposite
Ile Royale. The raid had been a success, and prisoners, together
with a large quantity of cod-fish commandeered by the officers,
were brought back to Louisbourg. When the prisoners were
released (they were extra mouths to feed), they carried back to
New England the news of the mutiny and details of the layout
and fortifications of Louisbourg.

For the first time, the New Englanders realised that the
formidable fortress might not be impregnable after all. They
were angered by the raid on Canso. They knew the French
had also been behind Indian raids on outlying settlements,
and that French privateers used Louisbourg harbour for shelter. The merchants saw a chance to demolish a rival in the
rich fishing grounds, and the ordinary citizens thought of the
fabled wealth of Louisbourg. Public sentiment was so aroused
that in less than ten weeks nearly 4,000 men had enlisted. On
24 March 1745, under their commander William Pepperell of
Kittery, Maine, a merchant of 'sound common sense and
sterling integrity', the New Englanders set out for Canso. The
whole enterprise had the aura of a Puritan crusade. Parson
Moody, appointed senior chaplain to the troops, went aboard
carrying a bible and an axe 'to destroy the altars of the anti-
Christ'. At Canso, they were delayed for three weeks because
of the drift-ice blocking Louisbourg harbour. This gave the
troops time for training and allowed Commodore Warren and
some ships of the British fleet from Antigua to join them.

The New Englanders landed with little opposition. A party
of eighty men, sent out from the fortress to join the forty men
guarding the shore, were too late to be effective. Soon after
landing, a scouting party captured the Royal Battery. The

45

retreating French had only spiked the guns, which were soon drilled out and used to attack the town. The siege lasted for forty-six days. During this time Pepperell did not find it easy to maintain discipline. His volunteers, bored with daily routine, went off on looting forays, often several miles from Louisbourg. Even the killing and scalping of nineteen of them did nothing to discourage these expeditions. When 400 men volunteered to storm the Island Battery, they refused the officers assigned to them, insisting on their right to select their own officers. Just as the raiding party was about to storm the walls, a drunken soldier let out a loud 'Hurrah', alerting the enemy and costing the lives of 189 volunteers.

To their own supply of artillery and that captured from the enemy, the New Englanders were able to add thirty cannon raised from the harbour. Under the constant barrage, morale was poor inside the fortress. Governor Du Chambon, who had succeeded Du Quesnel, praised the devotion of both soldiers and civilians who worked steadily 'without sleeping at night and, during the day, not daring to lie down anywhere lest the enemy cannon, which could aim anywhere in the town, fire upon them'. Powder was in short supply, and so was food. Finally, on 15 June 1745, Du Chambon asked for a cease-fire and two days later signed the Articles of Capitulation.

The New Englanders were not happy with the results of the surrender. The French had been allowed to take out their own belongings and Intendant Bigot had removed the contents of the treasury disguised as personal property. Government property was confiscated and sold; the proceeds were divided among the troops and individual shares were small. By keeping the French flag flying over Louisbourg and luring French cargo ships into the harbour, rich booty was acquired and this was divided among the British sailors. Since no garrison from Britain was available, the New Englanders had to stay till the following May. More than 800 died of fever and dysentery, and were buried in the cemetery at Rochefort Point.

Historians have called Louisbourg 'the cradle of the United States', and in doing so they do not exaggerate. In fighting together against a common European enemy who was deeply and magnificently entrenched on North American soil and yet had been easily routed, the New Englanders discovered new strengths. Resentment at the shabby treatment they had received from the British and pride in discovering that they were more than a match for trained soldiers dominated the feelings of returning volunteers. Their resentment increased when in 1748 the British handed Louisbourg back to the French. To the New Englanders it seemed as if all their work and suffering had been for nothing. These were some of the emotions that were later to erupt into the American War of Independence. Lt-Col Richard Gridley who planned the siege works at Louisbourg laid out the trench system at Bunker Hill. There were other Louisbourg veterans at the Battle of Bunker Hill, and by a strange coincidence it was fought on the thirtieth anniversary of the first siege of Louisbourg.

The second siege of Louisbourg in 1758 was part of a campaign by Britain to take Canada from the French. The Seven Years War, which had begun in 1756, widened into a colonial and naval war between France and Britain. Before attempting an attack on Quebec, the British had to capture Louisbourg. Governor Augustin de Drucour was far more efficient and level-headed than Du Quesnel and Du Chambon, but he was plagued with the same problems—lack of artillery and powder and insufficient supplies to withstand a siege. The British army was under the command of Lord Jeffrey Amherst, one of whose brigadiers was a brilliant young soldier, James Wolfe. He led the campaign against Quebec in the following year, and died on the battlefield of the Plains of Abraham.

Britain's combined land and sea forces outnumbered the French by about three to one. The landing, led by Wolfe, was made at Kennington Cove, to the west of Louisbourg, on 8 June. Only a few troops were guarding the coast; the majority

47

were occupied in preparing the fortress for a siege. Wolfe took over the Island Battery, and eventually the fortress was encircled by bombarding artillery. De Drucour knew that all he could hope to do was to hold out long enough to prevent the British from advancing on Quebec that year. In this he succeeded, helped by the gallant Madame de Drucour who, to boost morale, fired one of the cannons every day. After forty-seven days of siege, de Drucour surrendered. When the British marched into town, the officers handed over their arms as ordered by the Articles of Capitulation, but the soldiers broke their muskets over their knees rather than let the conquerors have them.

Two years later Commander Byron ('Foul Weather Jack'), grandfather of the poet Byron, arrived in Cape Breton with a hundred sappers and miners. They were to carry out the orders of George II, that the fortifications of Louisbourg were to be utterly destroyed. When the dust cleared from the final explosion of 17 October 1760, the fortress had gone.

By the Treaty of Paris in 1763, Cape Breton was ceded to Britain, and the same year was officially annexed to Nova Scotia. Britain's Board of Trade ordered Governor Wilmot of Nova Scotia not to make any grants of land on Cape Breton until the island had been surveyed. The survey was undertaken by Samuel Holland, who presented his report to the Lords of Trade in 1768. He described Cape Breton thus:

> Nature has blessed few Countries with so many advantages as this Island for the conveniency and number of its Ports . . . the general Fertility of the Soil . . . the quantity of Timber, the many Rivers, Rivulets, creeks Lakes Coasts &c abounding with Fish, the innumerable Game resorting here at different seasons of the year are such inducements as with a little encouragement would invite many to become Settlers . . . especially when it is consider'd that in raising of corn, Vegetables Hemp . . . and Flax in Lumber in Potash, but above all in the Fishery . . . the most avaricious would be satisfied and the most diffident embolden'd.

Despite the completion of the survey the British government persisted in its refusal to allow the granting of land. Not only did this discourage new settlers; it also caused the 707 people on the island much concern about possession of their lands and had already created problems about representation in the Provincial legislature.

John Grant and Gregory Townshend had been chosen by their fellow residents in Cape Breton County (which covered the whole island) to represent them in the House of Assembly at Halifax, Nova Scotia. When the two men arrived to take their seats, they were informed that, since only freeholders had the right to vote and since there were no freeholders in Cape Breton, their election was invalid. The people complained to the Lords of Trade that they were overtaxed by the Nova Scotia Assembly, yet were denied representation. In 1770, a proclamation of the Assembly announced that the 'Isle of Breton' would henceforth be part of the county of Halifax and 'deemed to be represented by the members of the county'.

The policy of the British government was to keep Cape Breton as a base for the fishing industry and as a reserve of timber for the navy's shipbuilding needs. A fine of £100 was imposed on anyone, except fishermen, who cut timber for their own needs. This policy continued until 1784, when Lord Sydney was appointed Secretary of State for the Colonies. At this time, Cape Breton became a separate colony.

COLONIAL PERIOD

The lieutenant-governor chosen to supervise the new colony was Major Joseph Frederick Wallet DesBarres. Born in 1720 of French Huguenot parents and educated in Swiss universities, he moved to England in 1754. His military career brought him to Louisbourg and Quebec, and in 1761 he was sent to Halifax to work on the fortifications of the dockyard. Two years later he was commissioned to survey the coastal waters of Nova

Scotia and Cape Breton, a task which occupied him for the next twenty years and resulted in the publication of the *Atlantic Neptune*, a collection of skilfully and accurately executed charts and illustrations.

In 1784, DesBarres left England in the *Blenheim*, with settlers and supplies, to take up his post as lieutenant-governor. He landed at Spanish Bay, which he chose as the site for the capital of the new colony. The town was named Sydney in honour of the Colonial Secretary, and by the end of that summer it had been surveyed and streets laid out. A governor's residence, courthouse, blacksmith's shop, brewhouse and cookhouse were in varying stages of completion. In June the 33rd Regiment, under the command of Lt-Col Yorke, moved into their new barracks.

Cape Breton was ruled, not very effectively, by a council. During the lifetime of the colony, its residents made frequent requests for a legislative assembly, but they did not get one. In addition to frequent clashes with members of the council, DesBarres was constantly in conflict with Yorke, mainly over supplies. Yorke saw it as his duty to receive the supplies and to distribute them. DesBarres considered that since he was described officially as 'Commanding his Majesty's Forces in Cape Breton and its Dependencies', he should therefore be in charge of distribution. Each time a supply ship arrived, there was a contest of wills over who would get the supplies.

In 1787, DesBarres was recalled and Lt-Col Macarmick became the new governor, but it was not long before he too became embroiled in arguments and local feuds. After his recall in 1795, six lieutenant-governors held office during the next twenty-five years. The last was General Ainslie, who in a letter to the Colonial Secretary denounced the inhabitants of Cape Breton Island as a 'set of deceitful, unprincipled aliens, imbued with the Yankee qualities of the refuse of three kingdoms'.

While it was a separate colony, Cape Breton Island was

Page 51 (*above*) The Cabot Trail winds behind Cape Smoky on its way to Ingonish, on the north-eastern coast of Cape Breton; (*below*) gently sloping hills, abundant timber and lush meadows attracted early settlers to the Margaree Valley

Page 52 (above) A view of Louisbourg from the harbour, drawn in 1731 by the son of Verrier, the chief engineer; (below) a plan of Louisbourg made from a survey done in 1745 by Lt-Col Richard Gridley, who thirty years later planned the trenchwork for the Battle of Bunker Hill

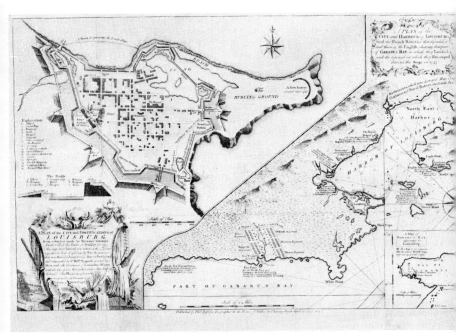

saddled with a host of officials. As Richard Brown noted in his history of the island: 'All the revenues of the Island, together with an annual sum of about £2,000 voted by Parliament, were swallowed up in the payment of the salaries of officers whose duties were in many cases imaginary.' In 1809, these salaries amounted to £3,475 2s od; the governor received £800. At that time, the population was about four to five thousand, most of them fishermen eking out a living, or settlers newly arrived, still clearing and breaking the land.

A crisis came when the Cape Breton court ruled that the duty imposed on rum was illegal. It was decided to re-annexe the island to the Province of Nova Scotia and formal announcement was made on 16 October 1820. The residents of Sydney reacted angrily and sent a strongly worded petition, signed by 500 freeholders, to London. Even as late as 1843, a committee in Sydney was trying to organise a petition to the Queen, requesting separate colonial status. Annexation brought with it many improvements. Agricultural societies which had been founded in Nova Scotia now spread to Cape Breton and brought farmers into contact with more efficient methods. The first one was formed in Sydney in 1820. The greatest benefit was stable government. The Cape Bretoners now had access to a legislative assembly through the election of their own representatives to sit in Halifax. The first two members returned were Richard Uniacke Jr, and Laurence Kavanagh Jr. Kavanagh was a Catholic, and royal assent had been given for him to omit the usual declaration against popery and transubstantiation, when taking his seat in the Assembly. Laurence Kavanagh was thus the first Catholic to sit in a British House of Assembly after taking only the State oath.

SCOTTISH IMMIGRATION

In 1774 the population of Cape Breton was 1,012, with not a dozen Scots among them. By the time the Surveyor-General

Crawley made a report in 1820, there were flourishing Scottish settlements along the western coast, at St Ann's Bay and around the shores of the Bras d'Or.

Richard Uniacke was rash enough in 1826 to venture the opinion that Cape Breton could absorb 1,500 pauper settlers. When the Surveyor-General learned that Britain was actually considering the possibility of unloading some of her poor on the island, he objected in the strongest possible terms. Cape Breton's harsh winter and 'stubborn forest' would be too much for the 'lazy inmates of poor-houses' to cope with, he wrote. Encouraged or not, immigrants, most of whom were Scots, poured into Cape Breton. In 1815, the population was estimated to be 6,000. By 1838, it had risen to 35,420.

The first Scottish immigrants arrived indirectly, most of them landing at Pictou, on the mainland of Nova Scotia. In 1791, a group of Scots arrived at Judique, via Pictou and Antigonish. They were later joined by a group who had come to Prince Edward Island with John MacDonald of Glenaladale. He had settled there with 250 of his followers, but when they learned that they were to be tenants instead of owning their own land, some of them left for Cape Breton.

In 1802, 299 immigrants, the first to come directly to Cape Breton, arrived in Sydney. Since it was too late in the season to plant crops, the council provided them with money which was to be repaid, either in cash or by work on the planned public roads.

A familiar pattern of Scottish settlement in Cape Breton was the development of communities by people from the same geographical area. Sometimes they arrived together, as in the case of the immigrants from Barra who founded Iona and Grand Narrows. Three hundred of them arrived in Sydney in 1817 aboard the *Hope* and the *William Tell*. More came as families or in small groups and were joined later by others from their home villages. Presbyterians from North Uist settled in Catalone and other places in the Mira area, while Catholics from South Uist moved farther to the south-west and settled in the Grand Mira district. Immigrants from Lewis settled largely in the St Ann's Bay area.

Because of internal squabbles and general administrative inefficiency, land granting during the colonial period had remained in a state of chaos. In 1821, Boards of Land Commissioners were set up in various localities and the settler applied to one of these for a 'ticket of location'. Up to 1827 land was granted free to settlers. One hundred and fifty acres were granted to each head of family and fifty acres to each child, the whole grant not to exceed the 200-acre free limit. Over this limit, the settler paid 5s for each fifty acres. Later a fee was charged for land grants. Before receiving his permanent title, the settler could, if he wished, join with others in a grant, and the fee was divided among them. Some settlers simply squatted on unoccupied land, without bothering to determine how to get legal title.

Even for immigrants who arrived with money and plenty of supplies, settling the land was no easy matter. It was essential that adequate shelter be prepared before winter set in, and the early settlers hated the dense forest that had to be cleared before anything could be done. It is not surprising that their New World Gaelic songs contain references to 'tall forest shutting out the sky from you', 'the gnarled forest', 'the tyrannous forest'. But at least the newly cleared ground was fertile and there was plenty of game. Even when food was scarce, and the winter wind howled and the snow piled in drifts everywhere, the weary settler could comfort himself with the fact that this was his land.

The Community at St Ann's

One of the most remarkable stories of early settlement in Cape Breton is that of Norman McLeod and his followers. Norman McLeod was born in Sutherland in 1780. At the age of twenty-seven he entered King's College, Aberdeen, to study for the ministry and graduated in 1812. During the next five years he found himself in constant conflict with the established Church of Scotland. In 1817 he sailed from Loch Broom with his wife and family, and a party of dispossessed Highlanders, for Pictou, Nova Scotia. After two years in Pictou he decided to move to Ohio, where he had been in correspondence with some Presbyterians. He and his followers built a ship which they named the *Ark*. In September 1819 McLeod and the men of his congregation set out to reconnoitre their new home; they would return later for their families.

They never reached Ohio. After rounding northern Caed Breton they stopped in St Ann's Harbour to fish and anchored there for the night. The following morning when they looked around them, they were so impressed with the beauty and potential of the place that they decided to go no farther. After each man had cleared enough land to put up the walls of a cabin, they returned to Pictou to pick up their families and additional supplies.

In December 1820, McLeod applied for a grant of 300–400 acres, and under his direction a settlement began to take shape. Soon St Ann's became 'the most sober, industrious and orderly settlement on the island'. In his leadership of the community, Norman McLeod assumed the role of a hereditary chieftain. The spiritual and moral welfare of his people was also McLeod's concern. In his deep commitment to Calvinism, he saw himself as one of God's elect, and it is not surprising that there was no place for any man strong enough to challenge his authority. But to those who accepted it he was protector, builder, magistrate, teacher and preacher.

McLeod's rigid conscience made him critical of even the most innocent vanities and his own wife was not spared his scorn. Once when she had purchased a bonnet with the proceeds from selling a piece of furniture, McLeod thundered from the pulpit, 'There she sits wi' a chest of drawers on her head'. Only once did he waver in his belief that all his actions were the expressions of God's will. He had sentenced a lad to have the tip of his ear sliced off for theft, and then learned that the boy was innocent. There was a long meeting between McLeod and the boy's father, about which neither ever spoke. Later, in refusing the offer of a Sydney lawyer to bring suit against McLeod, the father explained that it would be going against the will of God.

As the teacher for the community, McLeod did not accept compensation in money or produce. To do so, he felt, would make him a servant of the people. Instead, those fathers with children in school were expected to work on his farm as a fee. Many of the men in the community had prospered and could well afford the cash, and they found it particularly galling to be forced to labour for McLeod in this way. Nevertheless, none refused.

In 1848 there was a disastrous crop failure, and the government had to supply food to avert starvation. About this time, McLeod received a letter from his son Donald, the first in eight years, and learned that he was now in Australia. The letter and the newspapers Donald had enclosed were read and re-read by the members of the community and the younger people put forward the suggestion of going to Australia. McLeod approved of the idea immediately. He was now seventy-two; the famine had shaken his confidence in his ability to keep the community flourishing. Many meetings were held and about 975 people chose to accompany him, the majority of the community. Work was begun on a clipper ship, *Margaret*, and by October 1851 she was ready to sail. On the hillside above Black Cove, Norman McLeod preached his final sermon. Then those who were to remain bid farewell to the man who had guided their destinies for thirty-two years.

Although McLeod's domination of the community at St Ann's often fell little short of tyranny, he commanded an extraordinary affection among his followers. One man, after McLeod had been to say good-bye, took down his door and made another opening for it, so that no other man could cross the threshold after Norman McLeod.

INDUSTRIAL HISTORY

If many people came to Cape Breton Island to find a new life on the land, there were others with an eye for investment in the island's resources. The first printed mention of the existence of coal was in Nicholas Denys's book in 1672. Thick coal seams were visible in the cliffs between the Little Bras d'Or and the Mira Gut. Not until 1720 did the first coal mine begin operation, at Cow Bay (Port Morien). The first coal mine in North America, it was run by the French, and its output went to keep the workforce warm at the chilly and lengthy task of building the fortress of Louisbourg. When the French régime ended in 1763, coal mining continued to supply the British troops, and found a ready market in New England colonies.

Initially the British government was reluctant to allow coal mining on Cape Breton. On 19 March 1764, Brigadier-General Howe and some other officers petitioned the King 'being desirous of becoming adventurers in opening coal mines' but were refused permission. Three years later, the governor of Nova Scotia gave permission for mining coal at Spanish River (Sydney), but this resulted in a rebuke from the secretary of state who informed the governor that 'no more licences must be granted for taking coals from the cliffs in the island of Cape Breton'. DesBarres saw the mines as 'an inexhaustible source of revenue', and the government prohibition did not prevent a lot of bootleg mining going on. In 1820, the coal output was 8,000 tons, and fifty-two men were employed in the mines, which brought the government a revenue of £1,400–£1,600 a year. Even in 1819, however, 2,000 tons of coal were stolen from the island.

It was the debts of the Duke of York, brother of King George IV, that led to the establishment of large scale mining

58

on the island. His fortunes were severely 'damaged' in the early 1820s and his expenditures exceeded his income. There were rumours in England at that time of rich copper veins in Nova Scotia, and the Duke obtained a lease on all the mineral wealth of the Province. In exchange for a share of the profits, he transferred the lease to his jewellers, Messrs Rundell, Bridge and Rundell, who formed the General Mining Association (GMA) in 1825. On 1 January 1827, the GMA came into possession of the mines in the Sydney area and started mining seriously. That year, the GMA sold 12,000 tons of coal. In 1856, the company's production was 120,000 tons. By 1857, the Duke of York's estate had accumulated £54,000 from the mines and the GMA paid the Duke's representatives another £46,000 to relinquish all claims. After the lease was broken, any number of people tried to make a fortune at coal mining on Cape Breton. Between 1858 and 1870, twenty-one mines were opened.

The period between 1857 and 1893 was one when exclusive monopoly control of the coal industry was replaced by frantic competition. Each group of venturers had its own mine, its own town, its own transportation system, its own markets. In 1893, Boston financier Henry Melville Whitney took over a consolidated group of collieries on the eastern side of Sydney Harbour, and the Dominion Coal Company came into being, with almost feudal powers in the areas under its control. Whitney also controlled the New England Gas and Coke Company, and the Boston and Brookland streetcar line, and so had a market for his coal output. But the mines produced more coal than he needed, and tended to break up into small bits while being transported, forming slack coal. So, in 1898-9, Whitney founded the Dominion Iron and Steel Company (DISCO). There was plenty of limestone on the island, and the new company bought a part of the iron mine at Wabana, on Bell Island, Newfoundland. Soon ore carriers began to ply between Wabana and Sydney Harbour.

In 1901, a steel mill commenced operation at Sydney. It was well located near coal and limestone deposits, there was a large tract of land on the waterfront, the site was the terminus of the Intercolonial Railway, and the ice-free port of Louisbourg was only 40 miles away. From the outset, however, economics proved to be the crucial factor in operating the DISCO steel plant. Even by 1903, iron and steel from the United States were being dumped in Canada. And another steel mill had been established at Sydney Mines by the Nova Scotia Steel and Coal Company. A commentator noted that Scotia's growth was 'conservative yet regular', and that of DISCO 'spectacular but fluctuating'. From 1901 to 1921, the two companies operated within sight of each other, both getting their iron ore from Wabana and their coal from Sydney field. In 1905, Scotia expanded its steel plant, and by 1913, it was a major Canadian steel producer, vertically integrated from its coal operations to the manufacture of railway cars on mainland Nova Scotia.

Between 1893 and 1913, the number of miners on the island rose from 5,890 to 13,664. In 1915, the Dominion Coal Company produced 42 per cent of the coal output of Canada, operating fifteen collieries in Cape Breton, and two at Springhill. They employed 13,000 people, of whom 12,000 were housed at the mines. Nova Scotia Steel and Coal operated five collieries, and employed 2,200.

The Scotia steel plant at Sydney Mines was closed down in 1920, and production concentrated at Sydney. In 1921, DISCO and Scotia joined together to form the British Empire Steel Corporation (BESCO) and, in 1929, the Dominion Steel and Coal Corporation (DOSCO) came into being.

These years were marked by industrial unrest. In 1909–11, there had been a series of strikes in the mines. Both working and living conditions were bad in the mining areas of Cape Breton. The mines were deep, sometimes going down 3,000ft. At the Glace Bay Miners' Museum, the guides, who are former miners, recall brushing the gas out of the working with their coats, long journeys to the coal face, constant unpaid dead work setting up for cutting the coal, and heavy fines for unsafe practices. In 1908, at Port Hood, miners working with naked lights and loose powder as an explosive caused the deaths of eleven men. Colliery disasters were few in number. In 1911, there was a gas explosion at a pit in Sydney Mines, and eight men died. The worst disaster occurred at New Waterford, on 25 July 1917. Two hundred and seventy men were in the mine when an explosion ripped through the workings. Some hours later, ninety men were still missing and two surface workers lost their lives in rescue attempts. The death toll was sixty-five.

In 1920, the Duncan Royal Commission on the Coal Industry reported that 'the housing, domestic surroundings and sanitary conditions of the mines are, with few expections, absolutely wretched'. With the coal and steel industries in trouble, there was little incentive and less money to improve housing in industrial Cape Breton.

The most serious strike was in 1925. There was burning and looting, and it ended in violence. The newspapers reported that some of the striking miners, led by former war veterans, marched in an orderly manner to the Waterford power plant to urge the men there to come out. The company claimed that a wild mob was out to attack the plant. As they approached the plant, the company's mounted police opened fire. William Davis, a miner with a large family, was hit and died almost instantaneously. His funeral procession was a mile long, and even now Davis Day, on 11 June, is observed in New Waterford.

Bitterness still lingers in industrial Cape Breton, a feeling that the management is 'they' and the workers 'us', with incompatible goals. Times were hard until World War II brought prosperity again. The coalfields would last another 180 years, according to a 1941 survey. But only twelve collieries were producing in 1941 what twenty-two had done twenty-five years earlier.

A history of poor labour-management relations, of industrial and urban blight and exploitation still hangs over the land and the people, as is obvious even on casual visits to parts of Sydney, Glace Bay and other places in industrial Cape Breton. The steel mills were started to provide a market for coal mines owned by the same people. The problem of markets for the steel and coal has persisted through to the present day, and much of the future of the island depends on what happens in these industries.

3   COMMUNICATIONS

THE seas around Cape Breton are rough and dangerous. In winter, except around the south-west corner of the island, most of the sea freezes. Storms often break up the winter ice, and move it around. In spring, the ice from the Gulf of St Lawrence streams out through Cabot Strait. In summer, dangerous currents run strongly off the coasts, which are battered by gales. In striking contrast, the Bras d'Or Lake system is a placid inland sea with many sheltered bays. Until the 1850s, wooden sailing ships were common on these lakes, and around the island's coasts, and were only slowly replaced by small steamers. Up to the last decade of the nineteenth century, water transportation was the quickest way of travelling about within Cape Breton.

The French were alleged to be building two small warships in the Great Bras d'Or Channel when the British were besieging Louisbourg. To prevent them falling into the hands of the enemy, the French burned the ships at what came to be known as Man-of-War-Point. There was also believed to be a French shipyard on the Mira River.

Arichat, on Isle Madame, emerged late in the eighteenth century as a shipbuilding centre. In 1795, small ships of less than fifty tons, schooners and shallops, slid down the ways at St Ann's and Bras d'Or, while the first vessel was launched from Margaree. By 1811, ships of over fifty tons, decorated with figureheads or scrolls, were being built on the island.

Sydney Harbour was the site of a shipbuilding industry in the nineteenth century. The first sea-going ship built there, the brig *Nancy* of 101 tons, was launched in 1790. By 1900, approximately eighty-six sea-going ships were launched. Many were destined for the coal trade. Sea-going ships were built at Baddeck between 1821 and 1883; in 1853, fourteen cargoes of local cattle, butter, lumber, staves and sheep, with a total value of £7,000, were shipped to Newfoundland. Big Bras d'Or and Little Bras d'Or were the sites of other shipyards, and ships were also built at Boularderie, Whycocomagh, Little Narrows, Washabuck, Red Head, Big Harbour, Christmas Island, East Bay, and Red Islands around the Bras d'Or.

The men of Cape Breton followed the sea for a living if they found the life on the land unrewarding. Some sailed around Cape Horn to the sealing grounds of the North Pacific. Jack London's 'Sea Wolf' was alleged to have been Captain Alexander MacLean from East Bay, a seaman who left Cape Breton to hunt pelagic seals in the North Pacific Ocean and the Bering Sea. Before St Peter's Canal was built, Arichat was a convenient stopping place for sailing vessels, and at times was crowded with sails. Fishing, trading and a bit of smuggling all helped Arichat to prosper, and by 1830 the settlement was doing very well, with a booming shipbuilding industry and allied occupations (blacksmiths, sail making, lumbering). By the 1860s, Arichat, West Arichat, L'Ardoise and River Inhabitants were building graceful brigantines displacing up to 320 tons. But the increasing use of small steamers that did not have to wait for wind or weather, and the loss of life in the severe storms of the early 1870s contributed to the rapid decline at Arichat. The men left to join the New England fisheries and factories. Today, Arichat is a quiet and pleasant town, with neat houses and a splendid court house, looking out over an empty harbour.

After 1820 the demand arose for a canal at St Peter's to link the interior lake system with the Atlantic. But it was not until 1853 that a design was adopted. Work on the canal began on

7 September 1854. It was built by the Dominion and Provincial governments at a cost of $300,000 (£75,000). Work was suspended in 1856, and resumed in 1867. The canal was completed in 1869, and enlarged 1875–81, and 1912–17.

It is about half a mile long, 55ft wide; with a minimum depth of 17ft. A lock on the canal limits the length of boats using it to 270ft. From St Peter's Bay, small craft can slip around the northern coast of Isle Madame by using Lennox Passage. This narrow, crooked, shoaly channel is crossed by a horse-operated swing bridge at Burnt Point.

The Strait of Canso was an active area for shipping in the nineteenth century. Until 1860, Port Hawkesbury was known as Ship Harbour, and after 1901 coal from Inverness was shipped from a pier at Port Hastings. Gloucester fishing vessels on their way to the Gulf of St Lawrence regularly stopped at Port Hawkesbury for supplies and additional crew. Some of the Cape Breton Scots signed on. When the vessels returned to the Massachusetts port, the catch would be sold and the men paid off. Among the fishermen who then went on a spree were such well-known Cape Bretoners as Wild Archie (reputed to have paid $10,000 in fines to the town of Gloucester), Big Duncan, John the Weasel, and Donald from Bras d'Or (about whom a ballad was composed).

The *Mary Celeste*, then the brigantine *Amazon*, touched on Cape Breton's shores. She dragged ashore near Port Morien, was condemned, sold and temporarily repaired before sailing off to become one of the greatest sea mysteries of all times. Another mystery surrounded a raft of one million logs that left North Sydney, towed by a tug, in the spring of 1918. A North Sydney man had the idea of sending Newfoundland timber over to Britain this way, and he formed The Globe Timber and Transportation Company in 1917. The logs were cut in Newfoundland, and the raft was repaired at North Sydney before it, and the tug, disappeared for ever.

Sydney Harbour was a convoy marshalling point during

65

World War II. Between July 1940 and August 1942, 1,950 merchant ships sailed from here. Pleasure yachts tie up at Baddeck and fishing boats dock at Chéticamp, Louisbourg, Petit de Grat and the other ports. Supertankers slice through Chedabucto Bay; ships load gypsum at Little Narrows, and freighters pick up pulp wood and coal for export. In quiet bays around the Bras d'Or, rotting wharves stand as silent reminders of the great days of Cape Breton's shipping industry. In a bay near Baddeck, still visible under the water, is the hull of a schooner that sailed the seven seas, and cruised the waters of Cape Breton.

Ferries

Before the Canso Causeway was completed in 1955, the mile-wide strait was a bottleneck in island transportation. Travellers to Cape Breton, especially on night trains, were advised to fortify themselves with a shot of rum well before the long wait and the short crossing. This local method of preparing for journeys to the island and to Newfoundland still seems to be favoured.

When the railway was built across Cape Breton, the link with the mainland was through two vessels, the *Goliath* and the *Mayflower*, which pushed flat-bottomed scows across the strait. These scows could only carry two railway freight cars each. In 1893, the Intercolonial brought into service the SS *Mulgrave*, which pushed a larger scow holding a small passenger train on a double set of tracks. In 1901, the *Scotia I* came into service. This ferry could handle nine passenger cars or eighteen freight cars. She was joined in 1916 by the *Scotia II*, 300ft long with twin screws forward and a single screw aft. The ferries had to navigate through ice that streamed down from the Gulf of St Lawrence. For working in the ice, the *Scotia II* had a ram bow, and hull plates an inch thick. These two picturesque ferries continued in service until the causeway was built.

At the northern end of the island, fast modern ferries make

the trip to Newfoundland, from North Sydney to Port aux Basques, in about seven hours. From North Sydney to Argentia, on the east coast of Newfoundland a few miles from the Province's capital, takes eighteen hours. The first regular vessel to cross Cabot Strait (known as the Gulf) was the SS *Bruce*. She arrived in North Sydney on 1 July 1898, carrying fifty passengers from Port aux Basques. The Gulf is a rough sea passage, exposed to the open Atlantic in the east and to drifting ice and high winds from the Gulf of St Lawrence in the west. The *Bruce* ran aground on Scatarie Island in March 1911, and was lost. Two of the ships of the Gulf run, the *Bruce II* and the SS *Lintrose*, were sold to the Russians as icebreakers in 1914. From 1923 to 1949, the ferries were operated by the Newfoundland Railway, an agency of the colonial government.

The *Caribou* went into service in 1925. It was torpedoed by a German U-boat at 4 am on 14 October 1942. Of the 238 people on board, 137 were lost. Like a true Newfoundlander, Captain Taverner went down fighting. After the ferry was hit, the submarine surfaced. Captain Taverner steered his sinking ship towards it, apparently intent on ramming it, but the *Caribou* slid beneath the waves before reaching the U-boat.

Tragedy struck again when the *Patrick Morris*, an 8,360-ton Canadian National ferry, in service since 1965, was lost at sea in April 1970. The ferry had gone to search for survivors of a Newfoundland fishing boat, the *Enterprise*, off the northern tip of Cape Breton Island. The *Patrick Morris* was hit by a heavy sea, described at the official inquiry as 'exceptional', which, combined with the force of the other seas running at the time, apparently caused the stern door on the train deck to collapse. Water flooded in and the ship sank. The captain and three engineering officers were lost, but the rest of the crew, numbering forty-seven, was saved. No trace was ever found of the *Enterprise*, or of her crew of eight.

The terms of Union between Canada and Newfoundland in 1949 specified that 'Canada will maintain in accordance with traffic offering a freight and passenger steamship service between North Sydney and Port aux Basques, which . . . will include suitable provision for the carriage of motor vehicles'. In 1971, the ferries carried 244,354 passengers and 496,692 tons of freight across the Gulf. With the increase in the tonnage being shipped to Newfoundland, the operations at North Sydney were speeded up. Containerisation was introduced, and this and other changes led to the loss of about 500 stevedoring jobs at North Sydney in the mid-1960s. Of tonnage carried in 1971, only 59,455 tons were shipped from Newfoundland through North Sydney.

Lighthouses

The first lighthouse was built at Louisbourg, at the eastern end of the harbour. Made of fireproof cement and probably the first construction of this kind on the continent, it burned coal at the top of a tapering 60ft tower. Its light first shone on 1 April 1734. But ships continued to come to grief in the ice around the island. In 1828, the barque *St Charles*, with a cargo of dry goods, brandy, wine and gin, was stranded near Ingonish. In May 1832, the brig *Anna Maria* was struck by ice off Cape Smoky, and sank. In June 1833, the Sydney magistrates had 400 'destitute and starving survivors on their hands'. On 10 May 1834, the brig *Fidelity*, en route from Dublin to Quebec, was driven ashore on Scatarie Island; all but one of her 183 passengers survived. On the very dark night of 24 May 1834, the *Astraea* struck the rocks under Little Lorraine Head, between Louisbourg and Cape Breton. Only three people survived out of 251 on board. Local fishermen, despite their extreme poverty, undertook the task of clothing the bodies washed ashore before burying them.

It was this wreck that finally forced the various governments to take action. Lower Canada and the three Maritime Provinces agreed to co-operate in maintaining life-saving establishments on St Paul and Scatarie Island, and Nova Scotia

Page 69 Two contrasting life styles in the Fortress Louisbourg: (*above*) the elaborate bedchamber of Governor Du Quesnel; (*left*) the stark quarters of the ordinary soldiers

Page 70 (*above*) The governor's kitchen as it would have been in 1745; the planked ceiling prevented odours from escaping into the salon above; (*below*) a view of the Fortress reconstruction area, showing the Citadel and in the background, left, the Dauphin Demi-Bastion

appointed local committees to keep watch for shipwrecks on the coast of Cape Breton and to carry out rescue and salvage work. The British government offered to build lighthouses, if the colonial governments would maintain them. After 1839, when the lights began to operate from St Paul Island and Scatarie, the number of wrecks and lives lost was considerably reduced.

The 'Arrow' incident

On 4 February 1970, the oil tanker *Arrow* crashed on Cerberus Rock, south of Isle Madame, in Chedabucto Bay. She was carrying 108,000 barrels of Bunker C oil when she struck. The tanker, of some 18,000 tons, was under Liberian registry and had been chartered by Imperial Oil Company to carry its cargo to the pulp mill at Point Tupper. Heavy rains and south-east winds gusting up to 60 knots were reported when the *Arrow* hit the rock dead centre. Four days later, the ship broke in half. The stern section, containing about one-third of the cargo, sank in 90ft of water on 12 February. As the official report on 'Task Force—Operation Oil' put it, 'By the eighth day, 12 February, an estimated one-half of the ship's cargo of oil had been released and the calamity had reached catastrophic proportions. Out of the 375 statute miles of shoreline in the Bay area, 190 had been contaminated in varying degrees.' About 1½ million gallons of oil were floating around and sticking to the shores. The Task Force that the Federal Department of Transport assembled was faced with a unique problem: how to clean up heavy bunker oil in an area with icy waters, freezing temperatures and gale force winds.

In a short space of time, however, the Task Force cleaned up the shores of Chedabucto Bay, and pumped out the tanks of the sunken *Arrow*. The operation cost about $3·8 million (£1·5 million). Among other things, the Task Force planned, made and delivered the world's first washing machine for cleaning fishing nets. It cost $25,000 (£10,000), and was installed at Port Hawkesbury. The Canadian government's reaction to the disaster resulted in an improvement of the navigational facilities at the entrance to Chedabucto Bay; a 15 cents per ton levy on oil imported to Canada, to provide a fund for cleaning up oil spills; and stricter policies for controlling shipping and pollution around Canada's coasts.

Bobbing near the ocean terminal at Point Tupper is a small boat of unusual shape and design. It is a 'slick licker', a device used extensively for picking up oil on Chedabucto Bay. This 'oleovator' is a continuous terry-cloth and canvas belt that sops up the oil from the surface, then squeezes it out into containers in the boat. The oleovator laps up oil at the rate of about 45 gallons per minute. Light booms are also kept ready at the terminal to contain oil spills. One or two bad ones have occurred, but they have been quickly mopped up.

A footnote to the *Arrow* incident shows how some Cape Bretoners tried to take advantage of the disaster. Near St Esprit, sheep come down to the shore to eat seaweed. In April 1970, four sheep were alleged by their owner to have died from eating oiled seaweed. The Federal Government insisted on carrying out autopsies on the animals, which proved that they had died from worm parasitism. In the name of science, sheep were then fed Bunker C oil, but no ill effects were noted. The Task Force Report, in its solemn way, stated '. . . since external oiling may reduce the natural insulating quality of the fleece, and also its commercial value, sheep pastures were fenced off from the oiled shoreline as a preventative measure'. If the enterprising sheep owner received no compensation for his dead animals, he at least got some free fencing.

Superport and supertankers

Before the Canso Causeway was built, there was a steady flow of winter ice from St George's Bay into Chedabucto Bay. Ice still hampers the use of Sydney Harbour which, with depths of from 39 to 54ft, cannot handle very large ships. The Canso

Causeway created an ice-free deep-water harbour that has shifted the centre of industrial activity in recent years from Sydney to Port Hawkesbury-Point Tupper. The harbour is ten miles long, three-quarters of a mile wide, with a minimum depth of 120ft from the causeway to the Atlantic Ocean. It has a minimum controlling depth (ie the depth that allows ships to manoeuvre) of 90ft and can handle any ship now afloat—or on the drawing board. In February 1972, the 1,133ft-long oil tanker *Universe Japan* docked at Point Tupper. This was the largest ship ever to visit the western hemisphere, and the second largest ship afloat. *Universe Japan* drew 81½ft fully loaded and her deadweight tonnage was 326,562 tons. She discharged 2·35 million barrels of crude Kuwait and Iranian oil, enough to keep the Gulf Refinery at Point Tupper in operation for a month.

The contrasts between the old and the new in transportation and technology on Cape Breton Island were summed up by a resident, Mrs Catherine MacLean, in a letter to *The Scotia Sun* in the summer of 1971. After watching the 253,000 ton supertanker *T. G. Shaughnessy* dock at Point Tupper, she wrote, 'Twenty-seven years ago, as we sat in the one room school at Trout River at East Lake Ainslie, we were startled to hear the roar of machinery on the road outside. The teacher . . . confirmed that the first snowplow was going through the road . . . Trout River had been blocked all winter'. Trout River is only forty miles, in a direct line, from Point Tupper. Mrs MacLean noted that the *Shaughnessy*, unloading her 62 million gallons of crude oil, made 'a great deal less noise than did the old snowplow'. Four men operate the ocean oil terminal, and computers on the tankers handle the flow of oil from ship to shore. Even the largest tankers can be turned round in under forty-eight hours.

Lake and coastal steamers

While supertankers may incite awe, and treasure ships

73

avarice, the lake and coastal steamers of Cape Breton Island are remembered with nostalgia. The last boat to connect Sydney with Baddeck and Whycocomagh was the *Lakeview*, which stopped running in 1952. Captain J. Howard Beatty was the pioneer of the lakes service. It was he who ran the paddle boat *Neptune*, the first steam boat to enter the lakes in 1876. He died in 1883, when the *Marion* began a regular run from Sydney to Baddeck. His obituary noted that 'whether the most exalted in station or the poorest in the land took passage with him his kindness was shown to all alike'. The area north of Smoky also relied upon steamship service in the summer. The trips ran from May to November and were started by the SS *Acadia*. They continued with a line of boats named 'Aspy', the last, *Aspy III*, sailing in 1963.

Hugh MacLennan, the novelist, summed up the sentiments of Cape Bretoners about the small boats that were such a vital link between communities in an article in *MacLean's Magazine* in 1965. The whistle of the paddle wheeler *Marion* at Whycocomagh, which she visited three times a week reassured the residents 'that the outside world was just as crazy as ever'. The *Aspy* was the 'most wonderful' of all the ships, for she went to Cape North, and 'everyone knew that was as far as anyone could go'. In 1964, MacLennan found the *Aspy* again—tied up in North Sydney, a 'smokebegrimed wreck, her wooden beams rotted'.

The Mira River, curving through the quiet countryside for thirty miles, gives access to the southern Cape Breton County. In 1867, the first steamer was seen in Mira Bay. Captain Joseph Phillips, from Margaree, and his partner, Wesley Nicoll, from Fourchu dominated the river traffic on the Mira. Their first steamer, the 25ft SS *Juliet*, went into service in 1895. In 1913, the company acquired the 60ft *Avonlea*, a double decker, that could carry 120 passengers. In the 1900s, the Mira was a busy thoroughfare. The merchants along its banks depended on the river for groceries, feed, hay, coal, and bricks, loaded on to the local steamers at Mira Gut. With improvements in road transportation, the riverboat traffic was discontinued in 1958.

The MV *St Ninian* makes regular summer trips into the Bras d'Or Lakes, lying off Baddeck for a few hours on her cruises. In 1972, a pleasure boat the *New Shoreham* initiated a run from Warren, Rhode Island, to Yarmouth, Shelburne, Halifax, Isaac's Harbour, St Peter's, the Bras d'Or Lakes and Port Hawkesbury on a twenty-six-day 'circumnavigation' of New England, the Maritime Provinces and the St Lawrence water-way.

FLYING MACHINES

Cape Breton Island had the distinction of entering the air age and the electronic age before the island was well provided with good roads. It was on one of the bays of Great Bras d'Or that the first aerial flight was made in the British Empire and that some of the first experiments with hydrofoils for high speed water travel took place.

Baddeck is a quiet, somewhat sleepy village on the Trans-Canada Highway, forty-six miles west of Sydney. The harbour is sheltered by Kidston Island, and the V-shaped Baddeck Bay stretches two miles to the east, under the lee of the great head-land of Red Point.

In 1886, Alexander Graham Bell, the inventor, with his wife and two daughters, spent the summer at Baddeck. They climbed to the top of Red Point, and the view from the summit held them spellbound. In due course, Bell acquired the whole hill and Beinn Bhreagh (Gaelic for 'beautiful mountain') came into existence.

Flying kites was a passion with Bell. By 1891, he was con-ducting experiments with a flying machine based on the heli-copter principle. He wanted to get a man into the air, and at first kites seemed to be the safest way. He also believed that take-offs and landings would be safer from water. And so, year after year, in the soft summers of Beinn Bhreagh, kites took the air. In due course, a special sloping meadow was acquired and became known as the Kite Field. The Baddeck residents were baffled. A local boatman described Bell as 'fooling away the whole blessed day, flying kites, mind you . . . it's the greatest foolishness I ever did see'.

In 1906, Bell was joined in his foolishness by Frederick Walker (Casey) Baldwin, a Canadian from Toronto with engineering training, and by John Alexander Douglas McCurdy, the son of Bell's secretary, A. W. McCurdy, who was also the editor of the local paper, and an inventor in his own right (he patented a photographic developing tank and a film cartridge in 1906). The fourth member of the team was Lieutenant Thomas Etholen Selfridge, of the US Army, who came to Baddeck as an observer in August, 1907. Bell's basic idea for powered aerial locomotion was to equip a kite with an engine. In 1907, Glenn Hammond Curtis arrived to deliver a motor for installation in a man-carrying kite and agreed to join the team as the engine expert. The group was officially known as the Aerial Experiment Association.

On 8 December 1908, Selfridge 'flew' 168ft above Baddeck Bay on the giant kite *Cygnet*, the first recorded flight in Canada. On 12 March 1908, Casey Baldwin became the first Canadian to fly—10ft above the ice, for a distance of 319ft, in the *Red Wing*, at Lake Keuka, near Hammondsport, New York. Baldwin was the second British subject and the seventh person in the world to fly. The flight of the *Red Wing* was the first public flight in North America; the Wright Brothers' flights with heavier-than-air machines in 1903–5 were made in secret. On 17 September 1908, Selfridge was killed while testing a plane for the US Army with Orville Wright. He was the first officer of the US Army to die in a plane crash, and the first victim of a crash of a heavier-than-air machine.

On 23 February 1909, John McCurdy took the *Silver Dart* up over Baddeck Bay and flew 30ft above the lake for a distance of half a mile. This famous flight, the first by a British subject in Canada, and indeed in the whole of the British Empire, is commemorated in a plaque on a cairn in Baddeck's Main Street. The *Silver Dart* could be steered and had a wheeled undercarriage—both innovations in flying machines.

The Aerial Experiment Association, having achieved its goal of getting man into the air, was dissolved on 31 March 1909, only a year and a half after coming into existence. Bell called the aeroplanes 'aerodromes', and helped the first aircraft manufacturing company in Canada, the Canadian Aerodrome Company, to get off the ground, so to speak. Baldwin and Mc-Curdy stayed at Baddeck as assistants to Bell, and as independent 'aerodrome' manufacturers, building aeroplanes modelled on the *Silver Dart*. On 9 July 1909, the citizens of Baddeck were invited to view the newly completed *Baddeck No 1*. That summer, McCurdy and Baldwin flew some trials with the *Silver Dart* and the *Baddeck No 1* at the Army Testing Grounds at Petawawa, in the Ottawa Valley, about a hundred miles west of Canada's capital. Here, before a sceptical audience of journalists, both planes crashed—and with them the hopes for an aircraft industry on Cape Breton Island. Over 1909–10, the *Baddeck No 2* and the rebuilt *Baddeck No 1* were tested again and again; but, despite the fact that some great innovations in aerial flight had taken place, they were ignored by the larger world outside. In 1910, Bell closed his laboratories at Beinn Bhreagh and the Canadian Aerodrome Company suspended operations.

Bell's basic kite structure—using the principle of the tetrahedron—is now frozen in stone. The Alexander Graham Bell Historic Park faces Beinn Bhreagh and the museum seems ready to fly away at any time. In its roomy interior are artifacts and accounts of all aspects of the inventor's work. Among his many interests were hydrofoil craft, and here again Baddeck was the scene of many experiments with new and futuristic craft. Even before the attempt to establish an aircraft industry on Cape Breton slid into oblivion, Bell and Baldwin had started

77

to experiment with hydroplanes. The surface of Baddeck Bay from 1908 onwards saw a weird and wonderful variety of surface craft using hydrofoils. The basic principle behind them was to get a boat up to such a speed that it would ride on a set of wing-like surfaces (hydrofoils) attached to the hull, and skim over the water surface. Baldwin worked out the mathematical calculations and Bell supervised experiments. Bell saw the 'hydrodrome' leaving the water and becoming a 'hydro-aerodrome'—'the pioneer forerunner of a new type of flying machine'. In December 1911, Baldwin got the *HD-1* up to 30 mph on Baddeck Bay. On 10 October 1918, the cigar-shaped *HD-4* was launched and, on 19 September 1919, it reached a speed of 70·86mph over a mile course on Baddeck Bay. In 1920, officers from the US Navy and the British Admiralty watched the *HD-4* go through its paces but, again, official interest fizzled out. Bell and Baldwin had been too early with their aeroplanes to interest the military, and were too late with their hydrofoils. The *HD-4* was beached near Beinn Bhreagh, and lay there for decades.

Bell died at Beinn Bhreagh on 2 August 1922, but Baldwin continued the work on the hydrofoils, building high speed targets embodying tetrahedral cells. The culmination of his work was the design of radio-controlled, self-propelled targets which were tested on open water and ice on Baddeck Bay in 1942–3. Nothing came of these trials.

TELECOMMUNICATIONS

In January 1972, in a small settlement about nine miles west of Sydney, 'Progress Replaces Katie' as a newspaper headline put it. Mrs Katie MacDonald, a widow of over eighty, had run the telephone business at East Bay since before World War I. Apparently she was still using the original equipment, and the exchange was located in a room off Mrs MacDonald's kitchen. The Maritime Telegraph and Telephone Company

(MT and T) paid her a regular contract fee, and she recruited her own operators—her four daughters. In June 1972, MT and T announced a five-year programme of modernisation at an expected cost of $19·8 million (£7·9 million) and Mrs Mac-Donald was replaced by an automatic dialling system.

On Cape Breton a number of rural areas still have hand-cranked phone systems. The operator usually knows where people are, and will tell you that someone is away from home so there's not much point in ringing his house. Some people are still on party lines, even a few miles from Sydney, so that ringing phones are not answered automatically. And yet, Cape Breton Island entered early into the era of telecommunications, and the first telephones were installed nearly a hundred years ago. In 1877, the year after Bell invented his telephone, Gardiner G. Hubbard, later father-in-law of Bell and director of the company operating the Caledonia Coal Mines in Glace Bay, had two telephones installed in the mine, connecting the bankhead at the surface with the coalface below. This was the first known commercial use of the telephone anywhere in the world for underground communication. In 1878, the General Mining Association installed a telephone system, using a single wire about seven miles long, which connected the general office, the mine office, store and manager's office in Sydney Mines with the shipping pier office at North Sydney. This was the first group telephone system used in Canada, and remained in operation until about 1900.

The early telephone systems used different equipment, materials and operating procedures. The Union Telephone Company, organised in 1891, operated in Inverness and Richmond Counties, connecting Port Hastings, Port Hawkesbury, Grand Anse, St Peter's and Arichat. The Inverness and Victoria Company, founded in 1899, served Baddeck, Englishtown, North-east Margaree and Margaree Harbour. The Eastern Telephone Company operated extensively in Cape Breton County from 1890 onwards. On 22 April 1910, the Maritime Telegraph and Telephone Co was incorporated and began to consolidate the scattered telephone systems on Cape Breton and throughout mainland Nova Scotia.

Linking Cape Breton Island with the rest of the world involved another famous pioneer, Guglielmo Marconi. In 1856, cable links had been laid between Cape Ray and Cape North, and across the Strait of Canso, thus linking Newfoundland and Cape Breton Island to the mainland. In 1866, the Anglo-American Telegraph Company managed to lay a submarine cable between Newfoundland and Britain. Messages then went across the Atlantic, across Newfoundland, under Cabot Strait to Aspy Bay. From here the telegraph line crossed the island through Ingonish, Baddeck, Whycocomagh, and Port Hood, and down the coast to Plaster Cove near Port Hastings.

On 12 December 1901 Marconi, experimenting with radio telegraphy on Newfoundland, picked up the letter 'S' in Morse, transmitted from a station at Poldhu in Cornwall. Within a matter of days, a lawyer representing the Submarine Cable Company requested Marconi to dismantle his apparatus and to stop the tests, as they constituted an infringement on the company's monopoly of communication between Newfoundland and the outside world. Bell offered Marconi the use of Beinn Bhreagh for his experiments, but Marconi picked Table Head, near Glace Bay. From there, on 15 December 1902, the first public transatlantic wireless message crossed the Atlantic. Even before the Governor General of Canada, Lord Minto, could send a message to King Edward VII, the London *Times* correspondent at Glace Bay sent off the following:

TIMES LONDON. BEING PRESENT AT TRANSMISSION IN MARCONI'S CANADIAN STATION HAVE HONOUR SEND THROUGH TIMES INVENTOR'S FIRST TRANSATLANTIC MESSAGE OF GREETING TO ENGLAND AND ITALY. PARKIN.

In the winter of 1904–5, the Glace Bay station was dismantled and moved five miles away. A fire damaged the station in 1909, and a new station was opened on 23 April 1910. The wireless reception station was moved thirty miles south to Louisbourg in 1912–13, when simultaneous operation was started on both sides of the Atlantic. In 1926, with improvements in radio communication, the Louisbourg station was dismantled. Communication across great distances is now done by microwave. There is still a small community called Marconi south of Glace Bay.

ROADS

The Provincial government owns and maintains 2,750 miles of highway on the island; of these, 400 miles are classed as arterial roads, including the TransCanada Highway and the 100 series; 700 miles are Collector roads that are mostly paved, and the rest are local roads. In addition, there are roads in the National Park maintained by park staff. Even after a January blizzard in 1972, these park roads were cleared and sanded by eight o'clock in the morning.

Until after the middle of the nineteenth century, the poor roads on the island kept Cape Bretoners apart, especially in winter. The first road was probably the one built by Count Raymond between St Peter's and Louisbourg in the early eighteenth century. Settlement grew up along this road, where there were a number of fine farms, but it fell into disrepair. By 1800, there were no more than ten miles of passable roads in the island, and only in 1817 was overland postal communication established between Halifax and Sydney. An Indian did the trip once a month. After Cape Breton rejoined Nova Scotia in 1820, roads and bridges were improved, and in 1821, a weekly postal service between Sydney and Halifax was established.

MacKinlay's map of 1865 shows an extensive network of roads. Settlers had begun to occupy the areas behind the shores and coasts of the island, and the road network went along the coastal routes. The valleys of such rivers as the Mabou,

CAPE BRETON ISLAND

Inhabitants and the Margaree gave access from the coast to
the interior of Inverness County. Roads followed the shores of
lakes, such as Ainslie and Loch Lomond, which had attracted
settlers. Shorter roads led inland and serviced settlers on the
backlands. The roads shown in MacKinlay's map of 1865 did
little to break down the insularity of the people of the island,
who tended to stay together in their small pockets of settlement.
As a Cape Bretoner said, even in the 1920s and 1930s, 'you did
not drive by miles, but by time.'

Most of the roadwork in the nineteenth century was done by
voluntary labour, but towards the end of the century, 'statute
labour' was introduced. All males on the island between the
ages of twenty-one and sixty were required to perform two
days labour on the highway. At this time, the municipal
councils were responsible for highways and bridges. Between
1915 and 1920, the Provincial government took over all the
highways, and ended the requirement for statute labour. Even
up to 1957, most roads in the Margaree area had gravel surfaces, but in that year, Trunk Highway 19 (the Cabot Trail)
was surfaced.

Motor cars and trucks came into use in the Margaree area
about 1917–18, but it was not until twenty years later that
regular snowploughing was begun. On 10 November 1938, the
Northern Inverness Snow Removal Association was formed at
Margaree Forks, where the annual snowfall reaches 143in.
The Department of Highways granted their request for a snow
plough, which was of a slow moving caterpillar type, much
plagued by mechanical breakdowns and inefficient operators.
It ploughed the roads between Inverness, Chéticamp and the
Victoria County line some ten miles south of North-east Mar-
garee.

The northern part of Victoria County was another isolated
area, not served by road until the Cabot Trail was completed
in 1932. The Cabot Trail is a spectacular tourist route, looping
184 miles around the northern finger of Cape Breton; it is also

82

a lifeline for the residents of the area. The road carries telephone and power service vehicles, road sanders and ploughs, bread delivery vehicles and food trucks, school buses and trucks taking the products of the fish plants at Neil's Harbour and Chéticamp to market.

North of Smoky, traversed by the Cabot Trail, is a remote, isolated area, with settlements wedged between the sea and the edge of the plateau, or scattered in the river valleys, or along the north coast in Meat Cove and Bay St Lawrence. Until 1840, there was no mail service north of St Ann's. Communication was entirely by sea, but this was hazardous and uncertain in winter. A post office was established at Ingonish and once a week George McNeil, of Cape North, carried the mail on his back from Ingonish to Bay St Lawrence and back. By 1890, a horse and buggy was in use, taking the mail daily over Smoky, across Ingonish Ferry and on north.

Another problem on the island was created by the bodies of water that had to be crossed. In 1880, fifteen ferries were operating in Cape Breton County alone. In 1920, the island's ferry service was placed under the Provincial Highways Board. Only three ferries now operate. The construction in 1961 of the Seal Island (or Big Bras d'Or) Bridge eliminated the need for the ferries at Big Harbour-Ross Ferry and at New Campbelltown. The ferries operate twenty-four hours a day, and fees are nominal. The Little Narrows ferry can be avoided by turning off the TransCanada Highway about three miles before Whycocomagh, and then following a somewhat rough and bumpy unpaved road along the edge of the lake, and thus connecting with the paved highway that links Little Narrows with Iona. The Englishtown ferry can be avoided by following the Cabot Trail where it goes up the valley of the Barachois River.

The Cabot Trail was paved, reconstructed and hardsurfaced between 1954 and 1961. Since 1957 the policy of the Provincial government has been to get the rural population out of the mud and dust, and the present thrust is towards better roads for the tourist traffic. The road between Sydney and Louisbourg has been paved, rerouted and reconstructed to handle the heavy tourist traffic to Fortress Louisbourg. The Department of Highways is proceeding with the paving of the Marble Mountain loop and West Bay loop, the Gabarus-Fourchu road, and the roads from Louisbourg to Main-a-Dieu, and from Cape North to Bay St Lawrence in the extreme northern tip of Victoria County. Beyond Bay St Lawrence is the small settlement of Meat Cove, reached only by a rough road; here the road network of Cape Breton Island really comes to a full stop.

RAILWAYS

While the roads on Cape Breton are being upgraded and improved, the railways, like those elsewhere in Canada, seem to have embarked on a programme aimed at deterring passengers from using them. Only one of the three Canadian National Railway lines on Cape Breton now carries passengers. This is the line that crosses the Canso Causeway and passes through Port Hawkesbury, Orangedale, Iona and along the southeastern shore of St Andrew's Channel to North Sydney and Sydney. This railway uses Cape Breton Island as a link between the mainland of Canada and Newfoundland. The two other Canadian National Railway lines on the island carry freight. One follows the coast to Inverness after crossing the Canso Causeway and carries freight twice a week. Another line to St Peter's has freight trains only once a week. There is also a network of railways operated by DEVCO for its coal mines.

The first railways in Cape Breton were modest undertakings. Small lines served the coalmining areas in the early days, and in 1854, the General Mining Association rebuilt its horse tramway between Sydney Mines and North Sydney, and imported two locomotives from England. This was the second real railway in Nova Scotia; the first had been introduced by the GMA in 1839 into their Pictou operations. In due course, industrial Cape Breton was criss-crossed with railways connecting the coal mines with the ports. In 1886, the GMA even built a railway engine, the *C G Swann*, at Sydney Mines.

In 1868 the Glasgow and Cape Breton (Nova Scotia) Coal and Railway Company Limited was organised and authorised by the Nova Scotia Government to build a railroad from Sydney Harbour to Cow Bay, via Bridgeport. In 1872, a railroad ten miles long, of 3ft 6in gauge, was built between Reserve and Sydney. This line used four Fairlie Patent locomotives, built in Bristol. The engine had a cab in the middle, and two boilers pointing in opposite directions so that the train could shuttle backwards and forwards between the pits and the shipping pier without having to turn round.

In 1874, the Cape Breton Coal and Railway Company, as it had become, began to build a line between Reserve and Louisbourg. This created a minor boom at Louisbourg. Scottish settlers flocked in from all over the island. A shipping pier was built, and a hotel, engine shed, blacksmith's shop and houses. This line closed down in 1882. The Dominion Coal Company was formed in 1893, and the Sydney and Louisbourg Railway, built by the company with a government subsidy in 1895, slowly began to rationalise the rail network in the industrial area. In Sydney, the Fairlie locomotives used to run across Charlotte Street, where the YMCA and the Vogue Theatre now stand, to a shipping pier. In its prime, the 's and L' carried more freight per mile than any railroad in Canada. As late as 1959, the railway employed 400 men, carried over 4 million tons of coal and had thirty-one steam locomotives on its thirty-nine-mile main line. At its peak, the s and L had forty steam locomotives of all kinds, including the largest of the Mikado class in Canada. Because coal was so readily available, diesels came late to the s and L. The first diesel switcher came into operation in 1960, and the last steam engine was retired in 1966. The s and L ceased operations in 1968, and the track has been taken up. In 1972, DEVCO sponsored a study of the railway line to see if it could be re-opened for tourist traffic. The railway station at Louisbourg, looking somewhat odd with only a short stretch of track in front of it, is now a tourist information centre.

An electric street railway was opened in Cape Breton in 1901. Its thirty-two miles of track operated in two separate sections, Sydney-Glace Bay and North Sydney, which were connected by ferry. The service was employee-owned after 1933, and ended its operations in 1947.

Serious attempts to link Cape Breton to the rest of Canada by rail began in 1885, when traverses were run on both sides of the Bras d'Or Lakes. The Eastern Extension, or Halifax and Cape Breton Railway as it was officially named, reached Mulgrave in 1880. From here the tug *Norwegian* carried passengers and freight across the Strait of Canso to Port Hawkesbury. When the decision to build the railway across Cape Breton came to be made, there were three possible routes: the northern route through Inverness and Victoria Counties to North Sydney (now followed by the TransCanada Highway); the southern route through St Peter's to Sydney, and a compromise central route through Grand Narrows. According to island tradition, a senator invited Sir John A. Macdonald, the prime minister, to a political picnic at Grand Narrows, where Sir John was so impressed by the scenery that he gave the word for the central route. The railway was built in two sections: Grand Narrows to Sydney (the Eastern Section) and Grand Narrows to Point Tupper (the Western Section). There was a shortage of rock, and the stiff clay topsoil was saturated with floodwater, and became 'like so much pudding'. The railway followed a meandering course because of the terrain; the original plan showed 100 curves in 101 miles of track. A legend arose that whenever the line missed the farm of a government supporter, it doubled back to give him a slice of the right-of-way money. The Eastern Section was opened on 4 November 1890, and the Western Section five weeks later.

At the end of the nineteenth century, two famous Canadian

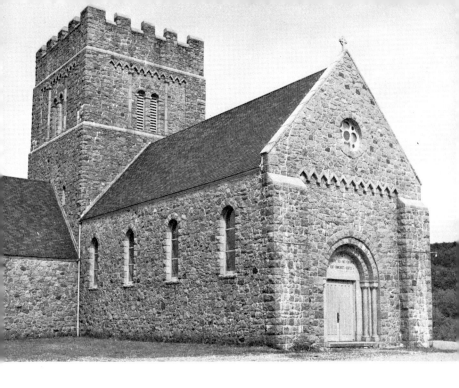

Page 87 Churches: (*above*) St Andrew's Catholic church in Boisdale, with its rugged look and Celtic cross; (*below*) the interior of St Peter's Catholic church in Chéticamp

Page 88 (above) The Union Presbyterian church in Albert Bridge overlooks the Mira River; (left) St Mary's Catholic church, with its tall graceful spire, is reflected in the water of Mabou Harbour

railway builders came on the scene. Mackenzie and Mann made a speciality of building railways—quickly, cheaply and badly. One of their lines, the Halifax and Southwestern (H and SW) came to be known as the 'Hellish Slow and Wobbly'. In Inverness County, the Inverness Railway Company had been formed in 1874, but it was not until 1898, when Mann got substantial subsidies for the line, that the railway started to become a reality. The line opened on 15 June 1901, and in May of the following year went under the control of Mackenzie and Mann, who also controlled the Richmond and Inverness collieries at Broad Cove. For its first thirteen years of operation, it had a thriving traffic and regular surpluses. In 1908, its peak year, the railway carried 322,000 tons along its sixty-nine-mile length to Port Hastings. But its operations were tied to the coal mines, and when they ran into trouble, so did the railway. In 1915, the railway defaulted on its bonds, and the line was in receivership until 1925, when it was sold to the Eastern Trust Company. Canadian National operated the line on a lease for several years, and then bought it in 1929. Mackenzie and Mann had promised to carry the line up to Chéticamp, but oddly enough, the rails never got past their own coal mines.

The Cape Breton Railway Extension Company, incorporated in 1884, planned to build a bridge over the Strait of Canso, and run a line to Louisbourg. The company opened thirty-one miles of track between Port Hawkesbury and St Peter's on 8 September 1903, but the railway went no farther. In 1920, it was bought by the Dominion government and added to what was then known as the Intercolonial system. Neither the Inverness line nor the St Peter's line has carried passenger traffic since the mid-1950s.

F

4

MAKING A LIVING IN
RURAL AREAS

ALONG the roads of Cape Breton there is evidence of a way of life that is slowly losing its appeal for the islanders. Long lengths of unpeeled logs lie at the roadside, waiting to be picked up and taken to the mill. Peeled logs for export are stacked up neatly at places like Iona, Baddeck, St Peter's and even at Point Edward, opposite Sydney. In the spring, lobster pots are piled up on wharfs in places like Grand Etang and Louisbourg. Fish plants line the main street at Chéticamp, and the small boats discharge their cargoes and head out to sea again. The farms on the island seem to consist of a house and a barn, a few fields where sheep and cattle graze, and acres of woodland. Beside some farm houses stands a yellow school bus; and outside depots are parked the graders and snowploughs for highway maintenance, which provide employment in different seasons.

FISHING

The seas around Cape Breton Island swarm with fish. It was these rich fishing grounds that first attracted the attention of Portuguese, English, French and other Europeans who used the island as a base. As early as 1606, some enterprising individuals were combining fishing with the fur trade on Cape Breton. Under the terms of the 1763 Treaty of Paris, the French were forbidden to fish within fifteen leagues of the coast of Cape Breton, and they faded from the scene. However, firms from the Channel Islands moved in quickly to take their place. By 1776, about sixty families were fishing from fifty shallops at Chéticamp. In 1774, the Cape Breton fisheries had 1,012 people using 121 shallops, exporting 26,010 quintals (of which there were about ten to a ton) of fish, backed up by six vessels with topsails and nine schooners.

The fishery continued to operate throughout the nineteenth century. In the year ending 5 January 1841, Cape Breton exported 44,807 quintals of dried fish, and 7,562 barrels of green fish. The Cape Bretoners had their problems, as they kept on the move to make a living. The *Journals* of the House of Assembly in 1842 noted that 'the Fishermen of the Republic' had not intruded in the past season on the fishing grounds of Cape Breton, but that in previous years 160 American ships had taken upwards of 30,000 barrels of pickled fish. These ships fished within half a mile of the shore. Between 1870 and 1890, American vessels were again operating around the coasts of Cape Breton, in pursuit of mackerel.

In the 1880s and 1890s, a number of small canneries developed around the coasts of Cape Breton. A lobster factory was built in 1896 at Kennington Cove, a small Scottish fishing and farming community a few miles west of Louisbourg. At Margaree Harbour, a man sent twenty-four 1lb tins of salmon to the Colonial-Indian Exhibition in London in 1886. The salmon were awarded first prize, and the man received a certificate and a medal which are proudly displayed in the Salmon Museum in Margaree.

There are basically two kinds of fishing in Cape Breton—the inshore and the offshore. The fish feed on the offshore banks in the Gulf of St Lawrence to the west and on the north-east Cape Breton and Canso banks to the east. Groundfish include catfish, cod, flounder, haddock, hake, halibut, and plaice. Pelagic and estuarial species include alewives, bass, eels, herring, mackerel, salmon, shad, swordfish and tuna. The molluscs and crustaceans include clams, lobsters, oysters and scallops.

At one time, the fishermen of Cape Breton had the distinct

advantage of being able to catch fish on their own doorsteps. At every place where a boat could be launched, a few fishermen would settle. But during the present century, the pattern of fishing has changed. Only certain places were suitable as harbours for the offshore fishermen, who used larger and larger boats and had to get their fish processed at larger and larger plants. The small fishermen's boats have been replaced by trawlers, draggers and Danish seiners. Although catches have still been rich, fewer fishermen have been needed. Employment in fish processing accounted for about 1,200 jobs on the island in 1972, the major centres being North Sydney, where 279 people were employed, Louisbourg (285), Alder Point (100), Chéticamp (112), and Petit de Grat (318). Forty people are employed at Grand Etang, and thirty-five at Port Morien, with a handful of others at Glace Bay and Main-a-Dieu. The fishing industry is characterised by a relatively small number of full-time fishermen using large boats, whose efforts are supplemented by a large number of part-time fishermen who use small boats. In 1970, there were 251 fishermen who worked more than ten months of the year, 715 who were employed for between five and ten months, and 1,178 who fished for less than five months.

For the whole island, the value of fish landed in 1970 came to about $6·8 million (£2·7 million). Lobster fishing remains a lucrative and individualistic pursuit. The bobbing floats that mark the location of the pots can be seen along the Canso Causeway and all the rocky shores of the island. Each fisherman has his own 'territory', although there is no legal basis for this. The need to conserve the lobster has cut down recently on this source of income, although in 1972, a bad and late ice year, when the season started about a month later than usual, one man at Margaree Harbour took three tons of lobster in a week, which sold for about a dollar a pound. Prices will be high when stocks are low, and this is part of the dilemma of the primary producing industries on Cape Breton, in which a number of people use fairly simple equipment to work the sea.

In the 1930s and 1940s, the harbours at Glace Bay and Ingonish were thronged with swordfishing boats—graceful craft with tall masts and long bowsprits. The swordfish were sighted from the mast-tops and harpooned from the bow of the vessel. But, in 1971, the American government banned the import of swordfish because of the high mercury content of the flesh. Over-exploitation has cut down on the number of salmon. Canada banned the commercial fishing of Atlantic salmon in 1972, but angling is still permitted. In 1940, 474 salmon were taken by anglers on the Margaree. In 1948, the peak year since records were kept, the take was 836 salmon. In 1971, only 116 salmon were taken on the Margaree.

An interesting project is one based at the Indian Reserve at Eskasoni, on the northern shore of East Bay. Here oysters are being cultivated by the Crane Cove Oyster Farms Ltd, which is run by the Indians. DEVCO is endeavouring to interest farmers and fishermen around the shores of the Bras d'Or in a similar type of development to supplement their incomes. They have established a Marine Farming Centre at Baddeck, and about twelve groups have been formed in communities around the lake. The oysters at Crane Cove are not resistant to the Malpeque disease, which produces a cancer-like condition in the tissues of the oyster, and a controversy developed in 1972 about whether to introduce disease-immune oysters or to keep the original Cape Breton variety.

AGRICULTURE

Land clearing and agricultural development reached its peak on Cape Breton Island about 1890. The small farmer, with limited resources, cannot improve his holding, and is soon forced off the land. The abandoned farm houses with gaping, empty windows, the collapsed barns, and the fields invaded by young trees are common sights on Cape Breton Island, even along the main highways. The best spruce trees come from abandoned farms, but the melancholy sight of land being lost to cultivation and of people quitting the land for the city contributes to the feeling of uncertainty about the future of the island.

In 1961, there were 1,975 farms on Cape Breton, occupying 12 per cent of the land. The farms varied from three acres to more than 560 acres. However, the improved land accounted for only 46,772 acres (15 per cent) of the 308,430 acres in farms. Although the farms averaged 156 acres in size, improved land accounted for only 23 acres, or about one seventh of the farm acreage. In 1966, there were 1,362 farms, but this number dropped to 640 in 1971. The farm acreage in 1966 was 233,204, but by 1971 almost 100,000 acres had gone out of farm use. Of the total 1966 population of 166,943, only 8,163 people were engaged in farming; about half of these lived in Inverness County. Only 768 people were employed in farming in Richmond County.

The good farming areas are at Boularderie, Bras d'Or and Point Edward, near Sydney, where urban sprawl is beginning to take farmland, and also down the Margaree. There are several large farms in the River Inhabitants Valley between Cleveland and Kingsville. In Richmond County, the farms are scattered along the main highway and elsewhere, while in Victoria County most of the farming is carried on in the Middle River and the Baddeck-St Ann's Bay district. Wheat was the staple of the early settlers, but this crop has been replaced by hay, oats, potatoes and, in Cape Breton County, by vegetable farming. Dairy farming is the most important agricultural occupation on the island. Most of the dairy farms are one-man operations with herds of about twenty-six milking cows. If a farmer has a milk contract, or can get established in a specialised market such as vegetables, he can ensure himself a steady income, and avoid the hazards of weather and markets. But all the small farmer can do is hang on until he retires or manages to sell the farm. Cape Breton is by no means self-

94

sufficient in food production, and food makes up a large percentage of the cargoes that roll across Canso Causeway.

Livestock numbers have decreased in recent years. By 1966, the number of horses on the island had dropped to 1,117. There are about 500 pleasure horses in the Sydney area, but these are not kept on farms. One of the incongruous sights on the island are delicately prancing horses, harnessed to sulkies, trotting out to exercise in the industrial landscape around Glace Bay. In 1966, cattle numbered 14,335; cows and milking heifers, 6,928. At one time there were 100,000 sheep on the island, and Cape Breton lamb was considered a delicacy. In 1966, sheep numbered only 11,960, of which about 8,200 were in Inverness County. DEVCO has expressed interest in aiding sheep breeders to raise lambs for the local market, and as a speciality for the tourist trade. Most of the island's 150,000 hens and chickens are concentrated in Cape Breton County, where seventeen commercial farms are engaged in poultry rearing. The Newfoundland market takes between 100,000 to 150,000 birds a year, but this will decline as the Newfoundlanders begin to supply their own needs.

The agricultural decline can be expected to continue on Cape Breton Island, and the abandoned farms may revert to forest or be turned into woodland to produce crops of trees. Some of the old farms are being bought by 'foreigners' (this includes people from the rest of Canada). Often what looks like an abandoned farm is an ancestral homestead that is still being retained, though the windows are boarded up and the house empty. In some cases, Cape Bretoners who live elsewhere in Canada or the States are buying up land for sentimental rather than economic reasons. Others, who see Cape Breton as a rural retreat, buy land with the aim of retiring or spending their summers there.

FORESTRY

Agriculture and fishing on an individual basis may have few

economic rewards, but it allows a man to be his own boss, which is important to a Cape Bretoner. The recent establishment of a large pulp and paper mill at Point Tupper has provided new sources of income and new uses for the land. But it has also introduced new standards of performance by an industry that has to operate profitably in a very unstable market.

As yet, there are no large areas of carefully planted rows of trees on Cape Breton such as can be seen in the Scottish Highlands. Balsam fir grows rapidly on the island, and will mature in sixty years. White spruce takes a hundred years to reach maturity, and trees such as red spruce, white pine and hemlock between 120 and 200 years. These softwood species, which make up 66 per cent of the island's productive forest, are cut extensively for pulp. But no one has discovered how to make good use of the hardwood trees, which take from 100 to 200 years to mature. Some hardwood is cut and mixed in with the softwood for making pulp and paper, but the bulk of it stays on the hills.

The forests are in a transitional stage between the original cover that was logged off by the early settlers (the first load of timber left St Ann's in 1818), and a new and well balanced forest that will supply wood for pulp and paper mills. The pulp and paper industry needs an assured supply of wood, and so must plan ahead. To the small wood-lot owner, or to the farmer with a wood-lot, his trees are his 'bank', to be spent if need arises. Some owners are good managers and skilled operators. Others are absentee landowners and older people whose wood is cut by itinerant loggers. Still others are untrained people who work their lots on a part-time basis.

The forested land on Cape Breton amounts to 1,780,000 acres, or about one-sixth of the total for the Province. The Nova Scotia Department of Lands and Forests has developed an excellent forest management programme, involving surveys and protective services. In 1958, the Province published a report on *The Forest Resources of Nova Scotia*, based on a forest inventory begun in 1952. Another inventory was begun in 1965, and was expected to be completed in 1972. In the 1960s, there were significant changes in the forest industries, which were able to achieve a higher degree of wood utilisation by a more integrated operation, and the use of chips. In 1965, the softwood stock was reassessed. It was estimated that there were 18,240,000 cords of merchantable softwood on Cape Breton Island in 1964, or about 22·8 per cent of the total for Nova Scotia. Hardwoods, on the basis of the 1958 estimate, came to 3,478,214 cords, or 21·2 per cent of the potential of the Province. Both estimates, however, may be 20 per cent too high, but this still leaves a lot of timber on Cape Breton Island.

During the 1960s, with the closing down of the coal mines, the production of pit props declined. In 1969, Cape Breton produced a little over a million cubic feet of rough pit props; most came from Cape Breton County. There are a number of small sawmills in operation throughout the island. In 1969, some sixty-four sawmills were recorded. Forty of them cut 100,000ft of lumber or less in that year. Only one sawmill, located at Glencoe Mills in Inverness County, produced more than 3 million board feet of lumber. This mill employed 18 people in July, 1972. Woodworking industries on the island only employed about 240 people at that time, and a number of these worked in building supply firms. The majority of the sawmills were operated by one or two men, supplying lumber for local markets.

Pulp and paper
The first industry to establish itself at the new Point Tupper superport was located to take advantage of the extensive stands of softwood on the island, and in the counties of Antigonish and Guysborough on the Nova Scotia mainland. In 1959–61, Stora Kopparberg of Sweden, one of Scandinavia's largest industrial enterprises, built a pulp mill at Point Tupper, at a cost of about $50 million. During 1969–71, a newsprint mill was added and

the pulp mill expanded at a cost of $86 million (£34 million). The mill has a capacity of 175,000 tons of bleached sulphite pulp a year, and 160,000 tons of newsprint. Nova Scotia Forest Industries, the operating company, leases 1,300,000 acres of Crown land in the seven eastern counties of Nova Scotia, out of 3,400,000 acres of productive forest land. The company also buys pulpwood from people who own wood-lots. Most of the production is sold in the United States. The mill is the economic mainstay of about 1,900 people in the area, although direct employment by the company was only 750 in July 1972.

This large undertaking, however, encountered marketing difficulties in 1971–2, when the slack world demand for pulp and newsprint resulted in a loss of $9·2 million (£3·6 million). The company's 1971 statement gave the annual sales as $18 million (£7 million); 109,400 short tons of pulp and 41,700 tons of newsprint were produced, indicating that the mill was operating well below capacity in that year.

Contractors cut wood on Crown land; they work with teams of from three to thirty men, each of whom can cut two to four cords of wood a day. A cord is a pile of wood, 4ft by 4ft by 8ft. Private owners also cut wood on their land and deliver the 8ft lengths to the roadside. Forty-eight semi-diesel trailers and sixty smaller units bring 95 per cent of the million tons of raw material to the mill. In mid-1972, Nova Scotia Forest Industries was paying $14 (£5.60) a cord for wood at the roadside. Most of the cutting is done by men with chainsaws, but the aim of the company is 'to get the chainsaw operators off the ground and into the cabs of harvesting machines'. In 1970, the company acquired two shortwood harvesters, which chew through the forest like science-fiction monsters. They fell the trees, strip off the limbs, cut the wood into 8ft lengths, load the sections and transport them to the roadside. Handling seven cords of wood at a time, they can produce twenty cords per man-day.

Under an agreement with the Provincial government, the

company pays them $2.75 (£1.10) for every cord of wood cut. The government then returns to the company $1.75 (70p) which is used for reafforestation. Wood consumption is 600,000 cords a year. In 1970, the company signed a new agreement with the Province which involved an increased cut, and an intensified silviculture planting that would require 200 man-years for its realisation, at a cost of over half a million dollars a year.

There is little or no silviculture on private land, despite the fact that the Province has a programme that will pay up to $25 (£10) an acre, for a maximum of ten acres, for work of this kind by wood-lot owners. Most wood-lot owners whose trees are cut by contractors receive $3–$4 (£1.20–£1.60) a cord.

Much of the future of the forestry industry on Cape Breton is going to depend on sustained yield from the woods, proper management and efficient operation by everyone involved to conserve, cut and replace the forest growth.

Over 1971–2, the export market for pulpwood declined and several hundred wood-lot owners and truckers had a bleak winter. The export market takes the short, peeled wood. Nova Scotia Forest Industries, which buys only 8ft lengths of wood, was apparently willing to buy wood from producers who normally exported pulpwood. But some wood-lot owners are resisting the temptation to become dependent on one large company as a market for their wood, and here again, the individual Cape Bretoner will have to come to terms with new realities.

COMMUNITIES AND CO-OPERATIVES

One of the ways in which Cape Bretoners have weathered the winds of change has been by co-operative action. Their activities on the land and sea and in the woods tended to isolate people, who were scattered all over the island in small settlements. The members of the Duncan Royal Commission of 1920 'were struck with the absence of community spirit and community enterprise generally'. In 1927 and 1928 the Mac-Lean Royal Commission investigated the fisheries of the Maritime Provinces and the Magdalen Islands. Its members heard of aging men, discarded gear, abandoned fishing vessels, and of fishermen who seemed to have lost the will and the spirit to put out to sea. One of the people who pioneered what came to be known as the Antigonish Movement and who had agitated for the Royal Commission was Father Moses Michael Coady, the 'Man from Margaree'. Born on 3 January 1882, of a family of farmers, he graduated from St Francis Xavier University at Antigonish in 1905, and from the Urban College in Rome, before returning to St Francis Xavier in 1910 as a professor. In 1928, he became the director of the Extension Department of St Francis Xavier University. In his writings and speeches he hammered at the theme that men, by community action and planning, could become 'Master of Their Own Destiny'. Between 1929 and his death in 1959, Father Coady dominated the field of mass education. When the MacLean Commission recommended the establishment of a co-operative organisation of fishermen, Coady was selected to organise the fishermen of eastern Nova Scotia.

At a meeting in Halifax, the United Maritime Fishermen was founded as a federation of local co-operatives. One of the main problems was the monopoly control that the fish buyers exercised at the wharf. In the small fishing villages there was usually only one fishbuyer, who also often ran the local store. If the fishermen did not accept his price, then they had nowhere else to go. The fishermen were often enmeshed in debt through a credit system on which they relied for their supplies. The fish companies that controlled the plants extended their operations to the boats. At Grand Etang, around 1900, there were thirty-two sailing vessels, with an average crew of four, all owned by the fishermen. By 1936, all but four had been taken over by the fish companies. The co-operative way provided an alternative for marketing fish for the men of Nova Scotia. During the 1930s and 1940s, with Moses Coady moving around the island, the fishermen came to see the advantages of co-operation, and organised co-operatives. In 1972, for example, the United Maritime Fishermen's plant at Alder Point and the Chéticamp Fishermen's Co-op Society each employed 100 people, and the Fishermen's Co-op Society at Grand Etang had forty on the payroll.

The fishing industry was only one aspect of Cape Breton life that was strengthened by the co-operative movement. Moses Coady was described as looking into the future, and seeing 'where the fog fell and lifted'. His cousin and mentor, Father Jimmy Tompkins, was the spark that started the drive towards adult education through co-operative action on Cape Breton. He wanted to see St Francis Xavier University at Antigonish serving the people of the region, and he was constantly on the go, prodding, probing, getting people to think about ways of tackling social and economic problems. At Reserve Mines, where he was parish priest from 1934, some miners told him they wanted to build their own homes. A credit union had been established there in 1933 (the first in Nova Scotia) and in December 1937 a co-operative store was started. With the backing of Father Tompkins, and the advice of a woman visitor from New York who had been involved in co-operative housing there, the men completed their houses in 1939. Thus Reserve Mines was the birthplace of organised self-help housing in Canada. At a total cost of $22,000 (£8,800), eleven houses were built, and they still stand in the area known as Tompkinsville.

Something of the spirit of the Antigonish Movement, and of its founders, is conveyed by a man who listened to Father Jimmy, 'When that little Father starts talking, he turns on a queer light back of his eyes, and the first thing I know I find myself wanting to go out and do something about the evil in the world.'

The legacy of Moses Coady and Jimmy Tompkins can be seen in the green, red and white 'co-op' signs that appear on the stores in even the smallest Cape Breton settlement, and in the strong credit union movement in the area. What began with fishermen soon spread to other areas of economic life. Co-operative housing schemes did a great deal to meet the needs of the people in industrial Cape Breton. Between 1938 and 1967, one hundred and sixty-three groups built 1,326 houses.

The Extension Department of St Francis Xavier University continues the work begun by Moses Coady and Father Tompkins. From offices in Antigonish, Sydney and Port Hawkesbury, it tries to put the resources of the university at the disposal of the people of the area. It has become involved with DEVCO's project for the development of the Bras d'Or Lakes, and has pioneered in social housing (renovating houses for welfare recipients). The Department also sponsors the *People's School* on radio and television, informing local people and getting them to think about the problems of the area and how to deal with them. Coady made the keystone of his approach 'the primacy of the individual', and built upon the Cape Bretoner's fierce sense of independence for collective social and economic action.

5   MAKING A LIVING IN INDUSTRIAL AREAS

BY the end of the nineteenth century, the land offered little to the ambitious sons of farmers with large families. They left for the 'Boston States'—the Cape Bretoner's term for the United States—or for Upper Canada, beyond the Maritimes. Those who wanted to stay on the island could always find employment in the booming steel and coal industries up to and during World War I. In the 1920s and 1930s, these industries, located at a distance from markets, were in serious trouble. World War II provided a temporary respite, but by 1960, it was claimed by the Dominion Coal Company's PRO that although the company had sold over $870 million (£348 million) worth of coal since 1939, 'it had not made a dime. As a matter of fact it had lost several million dollars.'

MIGRATION AND EMPLOYMENT

Cape Breton is caught in a dilemma typical of small islands that lie off the coast of large continents. While outsiders seem to have done well from the island, many Cape Bretoners have been forced to leave or risk remaining unemployed. The obvious qualities of the Cape Bretoner—friendliness, a sense of independence, and ability to work hard when the need arises, a sense of pride in the island—seem at times to turn to anger and a sense of futility that the island's potential has not been developed for the benefit of its residents. The advantages of Cape Breton can be summed up as an abundant labour supply; good training

103

facilities; beautiful scenery and excellent recreational potential; active efforts and incentives by various government agencies to aid development, and potential easy access to the markets of the north-eastern United States, though this is offset by tariff policies which work against the development of manufacturing in the Maritimes. The disadvantages are the geographical isolation, the remoteness from central and western Canada, the lack of a stable, diversified industrial base, and the unattractive urban—and in some places rural—environment.

NET MIGRATION

Region	1951–6 Number	%	1956–61 Number	%	1961–6 Number	%
Atlantic Prov	—37,800	2·3	—58,900	3·3	—103,000	5·4
Nova Scotia	—10,700	1·7	—22,900	3·3	—40,000	5·6
Cape Breton County	—9,000	7·5	—6,800	5·4	—11,000	8·4

Over the years, many people—usually the youngest and brightest—have left Cape Breton, leaving behind a population with a large percentage of old people and dependent children. Between 1921 and 1961, Cape Breton lost 57,369 people. Between 1951 and 1966, one person out of every four between the ages of 15 and 24 left the island, and most of those who left were between the ages of 15 and 40. Added to all this is the fact that the economic base is unstable, so even if a Cape Bretoner is able to get a job, there is no guarantee that it will last. In industrial Cape Breton, for example, only North Sydney and Louisbourg do not have a high percentage of their labour force in coal and steel. About one third of the island's total employment is concentrated in these two industries. When mines close, unemployment increases spectacularly in certain communities. Unemployment in New Waterford rose from 3 per cent in 1961 to 10·5 per cent in 1965, and in Dominion, the rate went from 4 per cent to 21 per cent.

Kenneth Bagnell, an editor of the *Toronto Globe and Mail*,

Page 105 Communications: (*above*) the ill-fated *Caribou*, torpedoed by a German U-boat while on a run between Cape Breton and Newfoundland, 14 October 1942; (*below*) the *Leif Eiriksson*, one of the fast Canadian ferries on the North Sydney–Newfoundland run

Page 106 (*above*) The ferry terminal at North Sydney; (*below*) view over Sydney, showing the downtown area and, in the background, DEVCO's coking ovens

wrote nostalgically of his home town of Glace Bay in 1970, 'The Evening Town I knew as Morning'. At that time, only two of the seven mines were still operating, and 1,100 men had been retired in the previous summer. Bagnell wrote of 'the ambitious young who fear the dark despair burdening so many who do not leave', and a local lawyer remarked on 'a feeling all around that subjugates you'.

Many men from Cape Breton have made their mark in the world beyond the island, including Angus L. Macdonald, Nova Scotia's most famous premier. And Cape Bretoners were always ready to go to war. Some fought in the American Civil War; others served in the South African War. In World War I, about 13,000 Cape Breton volunteers served in the Canadian forces. Cape Bretoners fought at the Second Battle of Ypres, Vimy Ridge, Passchendaele, the Queant-Drocourt Line with the 85th Nova Scotia Highlanders and other regiments. In World War II, the Cape Breton Highlanders fought their way through Italy and north-west Europe.

EMPLOYMENT IN MANUFACTURING (JULY 1972) (BY CATEGORY)

Steelmaking	3,200
Fish processing	1,193
Instrument making	932
Pulp and paper	750
Food processing	453
Light and heavy engineering	345
Woodworking	243
Heavy water	216
Quarries, etc	158
Ready mix concrete	124
Oil refining	123
Mineral processing	104
Printing	54
Auto assembly	52
Total	7,927

CAPE BRETON ISLAND

EMPLOYMENT IN MANUFACTURING (JULY 1972) (BY LOCATION)

		Main industries
Sydney	5,121	Steelmaking, instrument making, food processing, woodworking
Port Hawkesbury	1,211	Pulp and paper, heavy water, oil refining
North Sydney	363	Fish processing, engineering
Petit de Grat	318	Fish processing
Louisbourg	285	Fish processing
Glace Bay	117	Food processing
Chéticamp	115	Fish processing
Sydney River	100	Ready mix concrete
Alder Point	100	Fish processing
Little Narrows	50	Quarries
Grand Etang	40	Fish processing
Port Morien	35	Fish processing
Glencoe Mills	18	Sawmilling
Sydney Mines	17	Food processing

The two tables on employment in manufacturing show how narrow is the economic base of the island. The concentrations of employment in Sydney and at Port Hawkesbury are striking. In 1972, about 4,000 people were engaged in construction on the island; this occupation is a very seasonal one, and depends on the pace of the rest of the economy. In the coal mines and the steel mills, there is constant uncertainty about the future that seems to keep labour and management in suspense. In the mid-1960s, several hundred stevedores lost their jobs at North Sydney when new technologies for loading the ferries were introduced. As the new industries arising at Point Tupper-Port Hawkesbury show, new technologies require a few skilled people who are paid well. In order to cut down on the reliance on coal and steel for employment, the cry has gone up that Cape Breton must 'Diversify or Die'.

And yet, despite the depressed economic climate in some parts of the island, the feeling of uncertainty, and the high, localised unemployment, Cape Bretoners are not doing too badly financially in absolute terms. In the 1930s, some miners used to go to work carrying empty lunch pails. There was no bread in the house, but they were too proud to show that they were unable to earn enough to keep themselves fed. In 1969, the per capita disposable income for Cape Breton was about $2,041 (£816)—about $70 (£28) more than the average for Nova Scotia, but $350 (£140) less than the Canadian figure. Cape Bretoners have to balance the demands of the larger society for better economic performance to ensure higher income, while hanging on to their precious feeling that they have a better way of life—if lower incomes—than other Canadians.

THE STEEL INDUSTRY

Black Friday—13 October 1967—marked the turning point in the history of economic development on Cape Breton Island. On that day the Dominion Steel and Coal Corporation (DOSCO) announced that it would close its steel plant at Sydney by 30 April 1968. DOSCO's announcement sparked a 'March of Concern' in Sydney. Twenty thousand people marched from the gates of the steel mills to the Sydney Sports Centre in a demonstration of solidarity. After some hectic negotiations, the Provincial government formed Sydney Steel Corporation (SYSCO), took over the steel mills, and began a $95 million (£38 million) modernisation programme. This move created a spirit of optimism on the island. When SYSCO took over, the plant had a number of advantages. There was a straight-through flow from dock to finishing mills, the labour force was in a co-operative mood, and SYSCO was headed by a dynamic businessman. But much of the equipment was old, and the plant had virtually no domestic market for its products. Iron ore was being imported from Labrador and Brazil, and even coke had to be imported. On 29 December 1969, however, the steel plant poured its millionth ton of steel in that year, and set a new production record. In the year ended 31 March 1971, the steel mill's profit was $8,495,340 (£3,398,130).

The modernisation of the Sydney plant will involve the use of advanced technologies that require fewer, more highly skilled workers. In 1920, it took 2·5 tons of coal, 2 tons of iron ore, and 0·8 tons of scrap steel to produce a ton of steel. In 1964, it took only 0·6 tons of coal, about 1·1 tons of iron ore (mostly pellets), and 0·6 tons of scrap steel to produce a ton of steel. A study of steel making, carried out in 1967–8, concluded that Sydney did 'not possess actual or potential production cost advantages in relation to other actual or potential competitive sites in Canada or abroad'. The study also pointed out that since steel sells for about six cents a pound, the logical site for a steel mill is where the market is, not where the raw materials are. Successful steel making depends on a mill having a local or natural market area that will take enough steel to absorb the fixed costs of the mill. The whole of the Atlantic region in Canada took only 15 per cent of the Sydney steel production.

The future of the steel mill seems to lie in the development of a relatively small, very efficient mill for producing basic steel and rails. In July 1972, the steel mill employed 3,200 people, but in the past, employment has fluctuated widely. In 1968, 4,918 people were employed. A study done when DOSCO announced that the mill would close revealed that 83 per cent of the steel makers were born on Cape Breton and 61 per cent were born in Sydney. Now that the Province owns the mill, the whole development process has moved from the strictly 'economic' to the political and social fields.

COAL MINING

The coal mining industry has suffered some of the problems of the steel mill which takes the output of the pits. Between 1921 and 1966, over forty coal mines closed down on the island. The last three coal mines in Nova Scotia operate on Cape Breton:

Princess Colliery at Sydney Mines, Number 12 at New Waterford, and Number 26, just east of Glace Bay.

In 1965–6, J. R. Donald headed a commission to study 'The Cape Breton Coal Problem'. Its report stated: 'The communities, the company and the employees had become conditioned to the receipt of federal government support, despite the continued unprofitable nature of the operations. No incentive existed for either DOSCO or the Union to take the constructive but drastic approach which the situation demanded.' The report noted that DOSCO was ready to get rid of its coal interest, and concluded: 'As an outsider, one cannot but view the problem of the mining communities with anything but great sympathy nor can one fail to appreciate the traditions of Cape Breton, and the spirit of the local people; nevertheless, one is forced to the reluctant but overwhelming conclusion that no constructive solution to unemployment and the social needs of Cape Breton can be based on mining.'

THE CAPE BRETON DEVELOPMENT CORPORATION

The Donald Report recommended that a Cape Breton Development Corporation be established, 'whose responsibility shall be the strengthening and expansion of the Cape Breton economy through exploitation of its resources and promotion of industry'. The Cape Breton Development Corporation (DEVCO) came into being on 1 October 1967 with the following objectives: to stimulate economic adjustment and expansion on Cape Breton; to rationalise the coal industry; to promote industrial development and to improve opportunities for productive employment, in co-operation with federal and provincial development agencies. DEVCO is funded by the Federal government.

Recruiting for the mines has ended, and older miners have been retired. Meanwhile DEVCO operates the three remaining mines on the island. At Lingan near New Waterford a new mine is to be developed, which should go into production in 1974, employing 1,200 men, and turning out 1·5 million tons of coal a year.

DEVCO created an industrial park at Point Edward, opposite Sydney, and a number of footloose industries were attracted to the area. General Instruments of Canada, a subsidiary of an American company, makes radio tuners, coils and TV transformers. Canadian Motor Industries assembles about seven cars a day; this is the only Toyota assembly facility in North America. Strontium Products are produced from celestite mined by Kaiser Resources on the south shore of Enon Lake. DEVCO owns Sydney's only 'high rise', Cabot Tower, and the motel next door. They lost $673,548 (£269,420) on these two operations in 1971.

In 1971, a new president, Tom Kent, took over at DEVCO, and a new policy emerged. DEVCO offered Cape Breton municipalities help with sewer and water projects, provided money for the rehabilitation of housing, raised some of the pensions of ex-miners, bought new hopper cars for DEVCO's railway, initiated a mineral survey of the island, and tried to find ways of reducing the sulphur content of Cape Breton coal. Some of these projects were carried out in co-operation with the Provincial government. DEVCO also began to encourage sheep farming on the island, the development of the Bras d'Or Lake system (with the initial stress on raising oysters), and tourism (building a motel near the Highland Village in Iona). The possibility of whisky distilling on the island has also been mentioned. In DEVCO's approach, emphasis is increasingly being laid on the enterprise of Cape Bretoners, helping them to do what they can with what they have. In an interview in The *Cape Breton Post* in July 1972, the DEVCO President, Tom Kent, dismissed the belief that a 'few big companies should come in from the Outside' as 'a false approach to development'. In a speech to the Union of Nova Scotia Municipalities in Sydney in June 1972, Kent noted:

MAKING A LIVING IN INDUSTRIAL AREAS

I have been here for only nine months, but already I find myself dominated by the wish to look at every subject in terms of our Cape Breton Situation. Maybe there's some magic in the atmosphere that quickly gets into all our minds and convinces us that Cape Breton and its people are very different from everywhere else. Or perhaps it is just that our problems are so tough that they take all our attention.

THE POINT TUPPER-PORT HAWKESBURY
INDUSTRIAL COMPLEX

While industrial Cape Breton wrestles with the problems of economic decline, the new industrial area around the Strait of Canso superport tries to cope with boom conditions. Port Hawkesbury was incorporated in 1966 with a population of 1,866; this had grown to 3,372 by 1971. The small settlement of Troy, about five miles north of Port Hastings, had 118 people in 1966; five years later the population was 441.

The core of the industrial complex is the Nova Scotia Power Commission's Point Tupper Thermal Generating Station, which opened on 26 September 1969. It burns Bunker C oil to produce 230,000 kilowatts of electricity a year.

The Gulf Oil Refinery went on stream in the spring of 1971. All refining operations are controlled from a single control room. Crude oil comes in from the Middle East, the Persian Gulf, and Angola. After refining, half the output goes to the United States, and half to Canada; the jet fuel produced here supplies the Gulf fuelling operation at Kennedy Airport in New York. The oil comes in by tanker, and leaves by tanker. The refinery supplies the local industries, and its sulphur output is used by Nova Scotia Forest Industries.

What looks like a huge pipe organ in the industrial area is actually a heavy water plant. Heavy water (D_2O) is used as a moderator to slow down nuclear fission in nuclear power reactors. Canada has lots of natural uranium, and using heavy water as a moderator means that the uranium does not have to be enriched. Canada has developed a nuclear reactor called CANDU—Canadian Deuterium-Uranium—and a ton of heavy water is needed for every megawatt of nuclear generated power. The water in and around Cape Breton contains a higher number of parts per million of deuterium than elsewhere in Canada. Basically, the process of making heavy water consists of pouring ordinary water down a series of towers in which there are numerous layers of sieves. Hydrogen sulphide (H_2S) is forced up the towers, and the interaction between the two produces heavy water. It looks and tastes just like ordinary water—but costs $20 (£8) a pound to produce. The Point Tupper plant, operated by Canadian General Electric, began production in September 1970 and is rated to produce 400 tons of heavy water a year. Water is drawn from Landrie Lake, and emptied into the Strait of Canso.

The Nova Scotia Forest Products Industries pulp and paper mill makes up the other existing component of the industrial complex and employs 750 people. The other industries, despite their heavy capital investment, have relatively few employees. The Thermal Generating Station cost $18 million (£7·2 million) to build, and employs forty-four people. The Gulf Refinery could be run with a staff of only twelve people on one shift, but the total number of employees is 123. Maintenance crews of from 60 to 200 men are called in when needed, and work on contract. The heavy water plant employs 216 people.

THE GLACE BAY HEAVY WATER PLANT

In 1972, Canada had three heavy water plants either operating or being constructed. One was at Douglas Point, Ontario, and went on stream in 1972, with a planned production of 800 tons. The Point Tupper plant had still not reached its rated production. The other, located at Glace Bay, officially opened on 1 July 1967, but has not produced a pound of heavy water to date. In 1972, the plant area looked like a giant's playground, with sections of towers and rusting pipes and metal lying all around. After an expenditure of $120 million (£48 million), the plant was being partially dismantled, and a $95 million (£38 million) rehabilitation programme was underway. Originally, the Glace Bay plant was supposed to do at least two things —get Nova Scotia into the era of advanced science-based industries, and provide work for the unemployed miners. But something went wrong. The seawater used for the process corroded the innards of the plant, and there was a long string of strikes during construction. The stories about what really happened at the plant are numerous. Since heavy water is vital to Canada's nuclear reactor programme, the Federal government, through Atomic Energy of Canada Limited, stepped in and will run the plant in future. Production of heavy water is expected to begin in 1975, and the plant is expected to reach its peak output of 400 tons a year by 1978. Fresh water, drawn from MacAskill Brook, will be used, and about 200 people will be permanently employed at the plant.

TOURISM

The prevalence of foreign licence plates on the island in the summer months, and the new motels that have opened up in recent years, as well as the increasing sales of land to non-residents indicate that more and more people are coming to enjoy the scenery and the other attractions of Cape Breton Island. However, there is a looming conflict between those who favour industry as the basis for development on the island, and those who want Cape Breton to become a haven of peace and a mecca for tourists. *The Cape Breton Highlander*, in its editorial on 5 July 1972, said 'Talking of mining in the Lake Ainslie area is particularly unnerving, conjuring up visions of industrial blight in an exceptionally beautiful area and the prospect of more heavy shipping in the Bras d'Or.'

The tourist boom began towards the end of the nineteenth century, and Charles Dudley Warner's book *Baddeck and That Sort of Thing* is credited with starting it. The book, published in Boston in 1874, is now rare, a defaced copy selling for $40 (£16) in Halifax in 1972. How so trivial a book could have created so much interest is now hard to see. But the urbanisation process in Boston and New England made the island an attractive place for a quiet summer retreat. Baddeck lives largely on tourism, and advertises itself as the starting point of the Cabot Trail, which is one of the prime tourist attractions of Cape Breton Island. Indeed it may be *too* popular, and there are complaints that tourists 'do' the Trail in a day or so, and then drive off Cape Breton without pausing to investigate some of the other corners of this part of Nova Scotia.

Many of the tourists are self-contained. They come by camper or trailer, or carrying all their needs with them in the car. On the Cabot Trail, a sign in the North Aspy Valley points to the woods and says simply 'cold water'. Another, at Petit Etang reads 'Pleasant Motoring'. 'Free Tennis' is advertised at a court in Pleasant Bay, and at the entrance to St Joseph du Moine, there is a long list of free facilities.

In 1968, a survey of the tourist trade was carried out by the Province. Cape Breton was visited by about half the tourist parties interviewed. About half the tourists were Canadian and the rest American. In 1969, about 336,000 tourists spent an estimated $4,535,182 (£1,814,072) on the island. The number of visitors to Cape Breton Highlands National Park in 1968, based on traffic counts on the Cabot Trail, was 810,651. In 1971, the figure was 760,000, but a survey showed that 371,000 visitors actually spent—or planned to spend—time in the park. Fortress Louisbourg attracted 194,653 people in 1968, and in 1971 no fewer than 315,000 visited the site. Visitors to the Alexander Graham Bell Museum at Baddeck numbered 108,351 in 1968 and 210,000 in 1971. The Mount Smoky Ski Lodge, between Ingonish Ferry and Ingonish

Beach, opened in the early 1970s; the chair lift takes people up 1,000ft, even in summer, and the view from the edge of the interior plateau is spectacular.

DEVCO is attempting to promote tourism as one of the main underpinnings of the island's future economy. A full-time director for tourism was appointed in 1972. There is a Cape Breton Tourist Association, and the Nova Scotia Department of Tourism has a Group Travel Director based in Sydney. In 1972, DEVCO was planning to establish tourist information centres at North Sydney, Grand Anse, Whycocomagh, and Margaree, linked together by an island-wide reservation system for tourists. The tourist season—from June to October—is comparatively short, and operators must recover their costs over a five-month period. The president of DEVCO estimated that if the average visitor's stay in Cape Breton could be extended by just one day, the additional money spent would total $6 million (£2·4 million) a year. In 1972, a study was carried out to see if the Sydney and Louisbourg Railway might be re-opened as a tourist attraction. Grants have been given to the Mad Potters of Sydney Mines, a group of ex-miners who have developed considerable skill in making pottery depicting aspects of life in the collieries. DEVCO has also provided grants to Theatre on the Island, a troupe of touring players, and is investigating the possibilities of 'Bed and Breakfast' type accommodation. Sixty per cent of visitors come in July and August, but the island is lovely when the leaves are changing and DEVCO hopes to encourage more people to come in September and October.

6   THE SOCIAL ENVIRONMENT

POPULATION GROWTH AND DISTRIBUTION

THE population of Cape Breton Island rose from 35,400 in 1838 to 63,083 in 1861. At the first Canadian census of 1871, the island's population totalled about 70,000. Between 1881 and 1891, there was little increase in population. By 1901 the island population numbered 97,605 and ten years later it had reached 122,084; 95 per cent of this increase was in Cape Breton County, where the steel industry brought in people from outside and from the other counties on the island. The population of Inverness County, where the railway gave a new impetus to coal mining, increased from 24,353 to 25,571 between 1901 and 1911, but the populations of Richmond and Victoria Counties declined by several hundred. Cape Breton County has increased in population in this century, but now is declining slightly. The other counties have lost population, or remained the same. Only recently, with the Strait of Canso development, have the populations of Inverness and Richmond Counties begun to increase, and that of Victoria County continues to decline.

A similar pattern shows up in the towns. Sydney's population increased rapidly between 1901 and 1911, and has continued to grow because of its commercial dominance and location. North Sydney relies on fishing and transportation for its economic base. Its growth has not been spectacular, but its population over the years has steadily increased, remaining stable between 1961 and 1971. Glace Bay, on the other hand, is typical of the

118

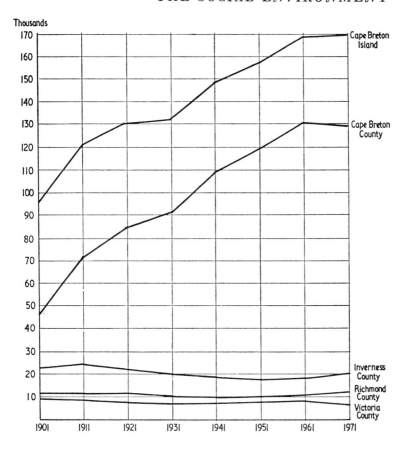

POPULATION CHANGES, 1901–71

coal mining towns whose population increased rapidly between 1901 and 1911, and is now suffering a slow decline.

The island's population distribution has a lopsided look. Cape Breton County, with a population of 129,075 in 1971, has 132 people per square mile. Victoria County, with a population of 7,823, has only 19·3 persons per square mile. While the Big Barren, twenty miles south-west of Sydney, is a completely

119

uninhabited area of forest, rounded rocky knobs and small lakes.

The level of urbanisation has remained high because of the concentration of population in industrial Cape Breton. Of the Cape Breton County population of 129,075 in 1971 only 40,221 lived in the rural municipality. Most of the urban development is concentrated in a narrow belt running along the coast, starting at Alder Point, about twenty miles north of Sydney, and passing through Florence, Sydney Mines, North Sydney, Westmount, Coxheath, Sydney River, Sydney, New Victoria, New Waterford, Reserve Mines, Dominion, and Glace Bay to Donkin, about thirty miles east of Sydney. This belt covers about 35 square miles, or 3·5 per cent of the total county area of 990 square miles. Elsewhere in the county the population is scattered in small communities such as Louisbourg, 1,582 in 1971, Main-a-Dieu (394), Port Morien (470), Little Bras d'Or (453) and East Bay (293).

The other major concentration of population on the island is around Port Hawkesbury-Point Tupper. Elsewhere the population tends to be strung out in settlements that line the main highways, as they loop around the coasts or along the shores of the Bras d'Or. In Richmond County, most people live along the coast from L'Ardoise, through St Peter's, Louisdale, and around Isle Madame. The eastern part of Richmond County is almost empty of people, except around Loch Lomond.

The northern part of Inverness County is another empty area. About 350 people live at Pleasant Bay, and the rest of the population is strung along the coast south of Petit Etang, and through the Margaree Valley. In the southern part of Inverness County, where agriculture is important, the 10,000 population is scattered. There are concentrations at Inverness, Mabou, along the coast road between this community and the Canso Causeway, and at Whycocomagh. In Victoria County about half the population is concentrated around Baddeck,

	Date of Incorporation	1901	1911	1951	1971	Peak population (decennial census)	Date
County							
Cape Breton		49,166	73,330	120,306	129,075	131,507	1961
Inverness		24,353	25,571	18,390	20,375	25,571	1911
Richmond		13,515	13,273	10,783	12,734	13,515	1901
Victoria		10,571	9,910	8,217	7,823	10,571	1909
Cities							
Sydney	1904	9,909	17,723	31,317	33,230	33,617	1961
Towns							
Glace Bay	1901	6,945	16,562	25,586	22,440	25,586	1951
North Sydney	1888	4,646	5,418	7,354	8,604	8,657	1961
Port Hawkesbury	1889	633	684	1,034	3,372	3,372	1971
Inverness	1904	NA	2,719	2,360	1,846	2,975	1941

Middle River and St Ann's Harbour. The other half is concentrated in the Ingonish enclave in the National Park, and in small settlements to the north—Neil's Harbour, Dingwall, Cape North, and Bay St Lawrence. The interior of Victoria County is empty, unpopulated plateau land.

LOCAL GOVERNMENT

Two themes run through the development of the island's local government: the quest for individual freedom and local autonomy (many Cape Bretoners or their ancestors fled from tyranny and limited opportunities elsewhere); and the search for a rational and economical way of administering an island with a wide diversity of life styles and scattered pockets of population, relying mainly on primary production and processing for a living.

During most of the nineteenth century, the political life of the island was pretty dormant. If people complained about anything, it was about road conditions. A report by the Commissioner of Crown Lands in 1865 lamented:

> Nothing has yet been done towards opening new roads, as contemplated by the Assembly . . . Very many of the back settlers have to travel from their homes over paths on which it would be impossible to use a wheeled carriage, often a distance of ten to twelve miles before they can reach a main road. Both in Inverness and Cape Breton counties I have travelled through settlements eight to twelve miles in extent, having no other communication than a trail or footpath leading from one clearing to another.

In the close-knit, kin-based isolated communities, 'government', unless it did useful things like improving the roads, was not considered a necessity. The Cape Bretoner, like other Maritimers, has a penchant for wanting to put some distance between himself and his neighbour, so as to have a little 'elbow room'.

Between 1820 and 1835, Cape Breton formed one county

Page 123 Ships and boats: (*above*) the supertanker *T. G. Shaughnessy* docks at the ocean terminal, Point Tupper; on the left is the 'small' tanker, *Gulf Canada*, 15,000 tons deadweight; (*below*) in contrast, Petit de Grat, Isle Madame; a picturesque fishing village on the south coast of Cape Breton

Page 124 Industry: (*left*) the oil refinery at Point Tupper during the eclipse of the sun July 1972; (*below*) miners' capes, helmets and boots have an abstract quality about them as they hang in the changing room at the Miners' Museum at Glace Bay

of the same name and had a sheriff. In 1824, the county was divided into three districts, and in 1835, these districts became separate counties. The north-eastern section became Cape Breton County, the southern district was named Richmond County, and the north-western area became Juste au Corps (which means 'Jacket'). In 1837, probably under pressure from the irate Scots settlers who made up most of the population of the central and southern parts, Juste au Corps became Inverness County. In 1851, Victoria County, named after the queen, was carved out of Cape Breton County.

In 1879, the County Incorporation Act swept away the system of local government by Quarter Sessions, set up in the eighteenth century. The main aim of this act was to get the counties to tax themselves so as to be able to pay for the upkeep of roads and bridges. Each county was to be incorporated, and a municipal council was to be formed made up of elected councillors who chose one of the number, called the warden, as chairman.

The towns on Cape Breton pressed for self-government so that they could tax themselves and borrow money. Sydney was incorporated as a town in 1885, under a special act, and North Sydney followed suit in 1888. In the same year, the Towns Incorporation Act was passed; this required a majority vote of taxpayers in support of incorporation before it could be granted. Over the next two decades there was a rash of incorporation on Cape Breton Island, as new mining communities became towns. Inverness, incorporated in 1904, lost its status in 1968 and was 'dissolved' after the main economic base of the community, the coal mines, closed down.

Local government is simple in three counties and enormously complex in Cape Breton County. Neither Richmond nor Victoria Counties has any towns, although each contains a village, and in Inverness County only Port Hawkesbury is incorporated. Cape Breton County contains a city and six incorporated towns. The county areas, outside the cities and towns, are self-governing 'municipalities' with elected councils. Inverness has fifteen councillors, Richmond County eleven, and Victoria County twelve. The county towns or 'shiretowns' (their official designation) are Port Hood, Arichat, and Baddeck.

Each municipal unit is independent of every other unit. There is no overall governing body for Cape Breton as such; the only agency with overall powers is DEVCO. In Cape Breton County the eight units that provide local government are facing a number of problems, and the need to co-ordinate local government in the Strait of Canso industrial area is beginning to loom large.

In 1968, the Extension Division of St Francis Xavier University at Sydney published a four volume report of *Local Government in the Changing Economy of Industrial Cape Breton* (the Finnis Report) which outlined some of the dimensions of the problems of an area with a declining and unstable economic base. Local government seems to have grown up in the county on a largely *ad hoc* basis. In 1964 a Cape Breton Joint Expenditure Board was created in an attempt to rationalise expenditure in the county. There is also a Cape Breton Metropolitan Steering Committee for the county, and a Cape Breton District Planning Commission. The Finnis Report painted a picture of 'citizen power' gone wild:

> . . . this region of approximately 1,000 square miles and 130,000 people is governed by eight municipal governments with eighty-six elected representatives, nine school boards with fifty-three appointed representatives and more than thirty *ad hoc* authorities not including the Joint Expenditure Board and innumerable committees. It is difficult to conceive of an area with so small a population that could be more overgoverned and where the structure of local government could provide so much fragmentation both geographically and functionally with so little opportunity for planning and development on an area-wide basis.

The report recommended the setting up of one single-tier

regional government for the whole county to be called the Cape Breton Regional County Council.

The plight of some of the mining communities was revealed in the report: 'Dominion resorts to deficit financing. Sydney Mines continues to operate only by the goodwill of a local bank to which it is hopelessly indebted. New Waterford is barely able to meet its bills or pay its staff.' Complicating matters is the fact that so many of the houses in the mining communities are in poor condition, and so do not yield high property tax payments.

If industrial Cape Breton demonstrates the difficulties and deficiencies of development and local government in the past, the Strait of Canso industrial area shows the shape of future problems. Here there are seven municipal governments. Three of them, the municipalities of Inverness and Richmond, and the town of Port Hawkesbury, are on Cape Breton Island. The other four—the rural municipalities of Antigonish and Guysborough, which contains the towns of Canso and Mulgrave— are on the mainland side. All are affected by the new industrial developments at the deep water port at Point Tupper. Most people live in Port Hawkesbury, in Inverness County, which within a few years had incurred a debt of over $6 million (£2·4 million) for the provision of municipal services. The real property tax from companies located in the Point Tupper area has been shared among the various towns and counties surrounding the Strait.

In 1969, a steering committee was set up to review local government in the Strait of Canso area and their report, published in May 1971, recommended the consolidation of municipalities on either side of the Strait of Canso and the establishment of an 'Island Side Municipality' to form one local government unit. This municipality would be a form of regional government with representatives from an Urban Service Area (Port Hastings, Judique, West Bay, Denysdale, Port Hawkesbury, Point Tupper, Louisdale) and from surrounding areas in Inverness and Richmond Counties sitting on one council.

As in Cape Breton County, little seems to have been done since the committee made its report. In 1972, people were still commuting from a wide area on both sides of the strait to work in the new industries, and housing was scarce and expensive in the town of Port Hawkesbury.

The Province has the usual array of officials on the island, most of whom are stationed in Sydney. Each county has a supervisor of schools, and the island is considered as a region for highway maintenance and construction. One forestry manager covers Inverness County and another covers the other three counties from his base in Sydney. Two agricultural representatives split the island between them in the same way; the one for Inverness County operates from Mabou. The Department of Development has one officer who covers not only the island, but also Antigonish County. For welfare services, the island is considered to be one region.

The Federal government also has representatives stationed in Cape Breton, and most of these are located in Sydney. From the Government Wharf here, a Fisheries Protection Service operates, and there are offices of the Departments of Agriculture, Consumer and Corporate Affairs, Indian Affairs and Northern Development, Labour, Manpower and Immigration, National Defence, National Health and Welfare, National Revenue, Public Works, Transport, Veterans Affairs, and of Central Mortgage and Housing Corporation and the National Film Board.

Politics

Cape Breton County has a radical tradition. The Canadian Commonwealth Federation (CCF), the predecessor of the New Democratic Party (NDP), the socialist party in Canada, usually presented a slate for election in the towns. New Waterford and Glace Bay have each had socialist town councils. The CCF-NDP elected members to the Provincial House between 1939 and 1963, and now the island sends the only two socialist representatives to a legislature east of Ontario. In the Provincial House elected on 13 October 1970, Cape Bretoners sent ten members of the Legislative Assembly to the forty-six member house. Glace Bay and Whitney Pier—the heart of industrial Cape Breton—returned NDP members. Two Liberals were elected in 1970—one from Inverness and one from Cape Breton West. The other six members were Progressive Conservatives. In the redistribution proposed by the Federal government in 1973, Cape Breton Island will have only two seats—an urban one for the Sydney area, and a rural one for the rest of the island. The members returned in the October 1972 election comprised two Conservatives and one Liberal. The riding of the Liberal member crossed the Strait of Canso and included Antigonish County and half of Guysborough County. This MP, the Hon Allan MacEachern, is often viewed as Nova Scotia's 'representative' in the Cabinet, as he is the only Liberal elected from the whole of Nova Scotia.

WELFARE SERVICES

The Provincial government is responsible for most of the welfare services; municipal contributions to welfare are minimal, and usually restricted to handouts to those in dire need. A Children's Aid Society covers the entire island, and the Family Services of Eastern Nova Scotia provide certain welfare services to the population. There are Family Services social workers stationed at Sydney Mines, Whitney Pier, Glace Bay, New Waterford, and Port Hawkesbury. The social workers covering the rural areas face a wide range of problems in a large territory; the Port Hawkesbury social worker covers Arichat, a traditional Acadian fishing village, and Port Hawkesbury, a booming industrial area.

In the old days, a system of self-help operated in the rural areas. In times of crises and need, the kinship system could be relied upon for support and assistance; the communities looked after their own. Two chapters in *The Highland Heart in Nova Scotia* which describes life at Washabuck in the late nineteenth and early twentieth centuries are headed 'A Free and Hardy People' and 'An Economy Without Money'. Hugh MacLennan, reminiscing about life on Cape Breton, mentions how old Mrs MacDonald, who brought eggs in from the country, asked his grandmother to step into the street to see how 'Himself' looked. As the author remembers the story, 'Himself' was propped up in the carriage in his best suit. He had been dead for fourteen hours. When Mrs MacDonald had got through delivering the eggs, she would deliver her late husband to the undertakers.

In the coal mining areas, there was a form of welfare state, of a sort that was common in 'company towns'. The coal companies looked after the men, in a manner that would now be considered paternalistic. Miners' cottages rented for $4–$8 a month, and the larger companies had good hospitals and doctors, paid for through the check-off system. There were no 'poor law' provisions in the mining towns, but the companies ran relief societies. The Dominion Coal Company's Employee's Benefit Society insured all workmen against disability or death from sickness and accident, whether arising out of the employment or not. Each member put in 50 cents a month, and the company added the same amount. A grant from the Nova Scotia government, based on the tonnage of coal, made up the balance. In 1910, a Workmen's Compensation Act was passed, but the Provincial government exempted coal companies at whose collieries relief societies were in existence. Such societies, of course, tied their revenues to the coal industry, and when the coal industry was in trouble, so were the benefit societies.

In recent years, in common with the rest of Canada, various self-help efforts have developed. In Whitney Pier, a Neighbourhood Action Committee builds and repairs furniture for the people on welfare. A social housing programme in Sydney rehabilitates old houses and makes them more liveable. In 1972, tenants' organisations in Sydney Mines and Whitney Pier began pressing for the enforcement of extensive legislation on housing and health conditions. *The Cape Breton Highlander* began to run photographs of the inside and outside of poor housing in the area.

Black Friday started pressure for social change as well as for economic stability. Shortly after October 1967, a Metropolitan Action Committee came into existence in Sydney. They organised a 'spruce up' campaign, followed by 'stay in school' and 'back to school' campaigns. The 'back to school' campaign was based on a centre that provided information on a wide range of educational opportunities available to people. In 1970, the centre, known as Metrocentre, received a three-year demonstration grant from the Federal Department of National Health and Welfare.

In their brief for the grant, the Metropolitan Action Committee stated:

> Our area of Cape Breton is a microcosm of North American industrial society. Our people are subject to all the pressures of that society even though sometimes deprived of its benefits—alienation of youth; a sense of hopelessness among many people, young and old; bafflement, frustration and even despair in the face of increasing complexity in day to day living; pollution of the environment; the growing helplessness of the individual confronted by big government, big labor, big business; the whole range of the ills that attack the human spirit in the age of technology . . . The fundamental need is to restore the average man's faith in the possibility of his having some influence on his own destiny, and that of his family and his community. People who lack that conviction—and their number is increasing alarmingly, especially among the young—lack the fundamental ingredients of citizenship, in fact, of humanity.

Metrocentre's major aim was to serve as 'a contact with all community services and to act as a catalyst for community growth; with the main areas of concentration information, counselling, referral and testing'.

EDUCATION

The education scene on Cape Breton reveals a number of stresses and strains because of the wide diversity of people, cultures and geographical environments on the island. There is a move towards greater efficiency through the use of amalgamated school boards covering bigger areas and providing a wider range of opportunities in larger schools at centrally located points. At the same time there are demands for an education that takes into consideration the cultural backgrounds of minority groups such as the Acadians and the Micmac Indians. An inspired teacher at the Breton Education Centre (a high school in New Waterford) has pointed a way to solving this problem with the existing resources. He has encouraged his Grade 12 history students to create their own textbooks by documenting the oral history of the area. The students interviewed miners and management who were involved in the great strike of 1925. Miners who survived the explosion at Number 12 Colliery at New Waterford told their stories. One student even identified a former rum-runner, and learned how prohibition in the United States had affected the community. The general handiness of Cape Bretoners with boats stood them in good stead in those dry years.

After annexation to Nova Scotia in 1820, Cape Breton came under the provincial educational system. In 1824, Laurence Kavanagh Jr surveyed the state of education on the island for the Provincial government and reported that there were only two regular schools, at Sydney and Arichat. He also reported a variety of arrangements for the education of children. At Gut of Canso, a group of families had banded together to support a teacher who was paid in produce and boarded free. At Strait of Barra and St Peter's, children were taught by itinerant teachers. In 1827 there were only six common (ie elementary) schools on Cape Breton, but by 1839 there were sixty-four, with two combined common and grammar schools, attended by eighty-one pupils. It was not until 1850, when a superintendent of education for the Province was appointed and one man made wholly responsible for the school system, that positive steps were taken to improve education. The first superintendent, John William Dawson, had the necessary missionary zeal for his task. When he went on a tour of inspection, he was shocked at the low level of competence displayed by many of the teachers. They received no training, had no official curricula to follow and in most cases had been licensed solely on the recommendation of a clergyman.

There were exceptions; Alexander Munro, who had arrived in 1839 to set up school on Boularderie Island, was a graduate of Marischal College in Aberdeen and had trained as a teacher at the Glasgow Normal School. He was accompanied by his wife, who was also a teacher. Superintendent Dawson was impressed by all he had heard of Munro's teaching methods and noted that, during his tour of the Province, whenever he found a teacher who had been a pupil at Boularderie Academy he was sure to be 'of more than the usual efficiency'.

Dawson put all his efforts into getting a Normal School established in Nova Scotia, and in 1854 an act was passed to set up such a school. It was located at Truro, about a hundred miles west of the Strait of Canso. But in 1857, education in Nova Scotia was still in a poor state. Of the 976 schoolhouses in the Province, about 600 were described as 'comfortable', and 171 as 'bad'. Some 186 were log schoolhouses, and these were mainly located on Cape Breton Island. The 'Free Schools Act' of 1864 made assessment for the financing of public schools compulsory, and thus, in theory at least, opened the school doors to all children. Under the Act, English became the only official language of instruction, and French was relegated to the status of an optional subject. In homogenous French-speaking Catholic communities like Chéticamp, instruction continued for a while in French. The school inspectors, though

English-speaking Protestants, were sympathetic to Acadians' problems. Eventually, finding competent French-speaking instructors became difficult, and the Chéticantins had a succession of English-speaking teachers, mostly candidates for the priesthood, who in turn had Acadian assistants. The School Act of 1902 permitted the use of French texts and language for the first five grades in Acadian schools. In 1908, the post of Acadian Visitor was created to assist the school inspectors in their assessment of the quality of Acadian schools. In 1936, an improved programme of French-language education was inaugurated. This extended full French-language instruction to the first seven grades and enlarged the scope for teaching in this language in the higher grades.

Originally the local school administration units in the rural areas were called school sections—geographical areas with a radius averaging two miles. In the 1940s and 1950s, rural high schools were established, serving a single rural municipality, or a large portion of it. In 1958, for instance, the North-east Margaree Consolidated School was built, and all the students from six former sections were brought by bus to the new school at Margaree Centre.

On 30 March 1970, an agreement was signed creating a new form of consolidated school board. There are a number of anomalies and absurdities in the school system brought about by the division of the island into urban and rural areas. The Finnis Report noted that high school students from South Bay, which is on the coast about three miles north of Sydney, had to travel right through the city to go to school at Coxheath, just the other side of Sydney River. Amalgamated school boards were established in the Province to get around such problems. The Northside Cape Breton-Victoria Amalgamated School Board is one of three in Nova Scotia. It is made up of schools in the towns of North Sydney, and Sydney Mines, twelve school districts in the County of Cape Breton, and all those in Victoria County.

The Royal Commission on Education, Public Services and Provincial-Municipal Relations—the Graham Commission—which began hearings in 1971 was told that amalgamated school boards had not solved all the problems of providing good education for students in remote areas. North of Smoky, for instance, there are five schools—at Ingonish Beach, Ingonish, Neil's Harbour, Dingwall, and Bay St Lawrence. None offers Grade 12 education or specialised services like counselling, manual training, music, programmes to correct learning disabilities, or adequate library services. Senior high school students from northern Victoria County had to attend school in Baddeck, boarding in the town. Other students had to leave home at 7 am on the school bus for Baddeck, and did not get home until 5 pm.

The Graham Commission received a wide array of submissions on their travels through Cape Breton Island. At Chéticamp, the Provincial Department was accused of ignoring the 'French fact in Nova Scotia'. Chéticamp has been designated as a bilingual district by the Federal government, as part of its programme to encourage Bilingualism and Biculturalism. But a social worker in northern Inverness County claimed that the official attitude towards French language education had produced a generation of 'linguistic bastards', who spoke French but automatically wrote in English.

At Port Hawkesbury, the Inverness South Teacher's Union discussed the need for Canadian content in school material. While they wanted the American material replaced, they expressed the hope that it would not be with predominantly Ontario material. The brief also urged that attention be given to Micmac languages and culture. An Indian woman from the Middle River band, however, suggested that children might be better off if they were discouraged from using their native language while attending school off the reserve. The Federal Department of Indian Affairs and Northern Development runs a school on the reserve at Middle River, attended by seventy-four children. Apparently they had a great deal of difficulty when they moved into the school at Baddeck, because of their poor knowledge of English.

In the field of post-secondary education, Cape Breton has a wide range of facilities, but they tend to be concentrated in Sydney. St Francis Xavier University began at Arichat as a seminary college in 1853. Before that there had been a boys' school, called a 'college' established in 1833. The founder, Father Chisholm, thought he could defray the cost of building his college by converting into cash a cargo of farm produce. He collected the cargo, chartered a boat and set sail for St John's, Newfoundland, in 1834. He was never seen again. In 1855 the college transferred to Antigonish, and in 1866 it was empowered to grant degrees. In 1951, Xavier College was created as a 'branch' of the main campus in Sydney, rather than as a separate and independent college. Friction has occurred between the parent campus and Xavier College; throughout most of 1972, a rough sign saying 'C B U' (Cape Breton University) hung over the Xavier College Student Union signboard.

There are vocational schools at Port Hawkesbury and Sydney, which take students after Grade 10; about 900 students were enrolled in these schools in 1971–2. In 1968, the Canadian Coast Guard College opened at Point Edward; it graduated twenty people in 1972. The Nova Scotia Eastern Institute of Technology also opened in 1968. This offers training at the post high school level in a wide variety of technologies—chemical, civil, electrical, electronics, mineral, mechanical, and business.

At Point Edward there is a Federal Adult Training Centre for unemployed people who need upgrading and special trades training. This Training Centre is the third largest single 'industry' on Cape Breton, after coal mining and steelmaking, in terms of the number of people involved. A maximum of 2,600 trainees pass through the centre each year, with peak enrolment between September and July of 1,286.

In May 1973, the Provincial government announced the creation of Canada's first 'humanotechnical' college on Cape Breton. This college would comprise the St Francis Xavier Sydney campus, the Nova Scotia Eastern Institute of Technology, and the Point Edward Adult Training Centre. The 'new college', to be built at a cost of $20 million, would have a capacity of 2,200 students, and be located on the Glace Bay-Sydney Highway, near the present site of the Technology Institute.

DEVCO initiated a programme of scholarship aid to employees who wished to upgrade themselves when they took over the ailing coal industry. One man, who started work on the Sydney and Louisbourg Railway at the age of seventeen and was employed there for thirteen years, graduated from St Francis Xavier University, and now works in the Industrial Relations Section of DEVCO's Coal Division.

Regional library service

When Father Jimmy Tompkins filled his front porch with books in 1935 and invited his parishioners in Reserve Mines to borrow what they liked, he opened the first 'public library' in Cape Breton. The 'People's Library' began to receive contributions from the educational funds of various co-operative organisations and, later on, a small grant from the municipality. Father Jimmy was a strong believer in the importance of the role of community libraries in adult education. He saw their future as information centres for economic and social rehabilitation. He felt that libraries should become the universities of the people, and he once declared, 'I want regional libraries because I want the people to be able to know a fool when they see one.'

The Cape Breton Regional Library was established in 1950, and now provides library service to the counties of Cape Breton and Victoria. The headquarters office is in Sydney, and the Victoria County sub-office is in Baddeck. There are now branch libraries in Sydney, Glace Bay, New Waterford, North Sydney, Dominion, Louisbourg, Reserve (the Tompkins Memorial Library), Donkin, Florence, Main-a-Dieu, Sydney Mines and Baddeck.

The Sydney branch, the James McConnell Memorial Library on Bentinck Street, is the main reference library for the region. On the rare occasions when a reference question cannot be answered there, the services of the Nova Scotia Provincial Library in Halifax are available. The Sydney branch has a special collection of material on Cape Breton and Nova Scotia that is open to the public.

The rural districts of Cape Breton and Victoria Counties are served by travelling libraries, called bookmobiles. In 1969, the Cape Breton Regional Library became the first system in Nova Scotia to institute householder stops. In Victoria County, with a population of 7,823 people scattered over 1,105 square miles, central meeting places for bookmobile stops were hard to find. Now if a householder wishes the bookmobile to stop he places a sign at the entrance to his property, and a halt is made there. Bookmobile users are delighted with the arrangement, and have started phoning others farther along the route to advise them of the bookmobile's progress, thus cutting down the waiting period at each stop. In 1971, the total circulation of books in the two counties, including books circulated at schools, was 407,762, for a total of 30,273 registered borrowers.

The counties of Inverness and Richmond are served by bookmobiles from the Eastern Counties Regional Library, with headquarters at Mulgrave on the mainland of Nova Scotia.

HEALTH SERVICES

Neil MacNeil, in *The Highland Heart in Nova Scotia*, states that people on Cape Breton were not in the habit of calling in doctors for minor ills. There were local remedies—hot foot baths for colds; Epsom salts for most other illnesses; sulphur

138

THE SOCIAL ENVIRONMENT

and molasses and the open air in the spring. A bizarre medical note was struck in 1852, when a woman at Lakes O'Law contracted leprosy. She died in 1864. Her four sons, her daughter, a son-in-law, and two grandchildren died of the same disease. People buried in the Loch Lomond Pioneer Cemetery seem to have died either very old or very young. Here there is a sad row of small stones: 'Finlay R. 1895–1898'; 'Carrie F. 1895–1898'; 'Rory F. 1883–1894'.

Up to about 1925, the nearest hospitals to North-east Margaree were in the Sydney area and at Antigonish. Patients requiring operations or special treatment had to be taken over rough roads to Inverness station, and from there by train to hospital. After 1925, two hospitals were opened in Inverness; in 1931, the Daughters of Jesus opened a twelve-bed hospital at Chéticamp. A forty-bed hospital was opened here in May 1938. Rough roads in summer and snow in winter made travel difficult and painful for the patients.

The company town situation in the coal mining areas has left too many hospital beds in certain places and a lack of medical services in others. In 1970–1, health expenditure on Cape Breton Island totalled $26,057,000 (£10,422,800). Of this amount, $19,565,000 (£7,826,000) was accounted for by hospital costs, $5,856,000 (£2,342,000) by Medicare and only $636,000 (£254,000) for public health. On 1 January 1959, Nova Scotia initiated a National Hospital Insurance Plan, financed roughly fifty–fifty by a 7 per cent sales tax and by the Federal government. On 1 April 1969, Nova Scotia entered the Federal medical care insurance scheme (Medicare). This is financed mainly by the Federal government and by the Health Tax. These two programmes, which provide basic health care for everyone in the Province, have thrust the island into a new era of medicine.

There are major gaps in the health services on the island. The Public Health Laboratory in Sydney covers only 25 per cent of the required services; there is a shortage of dentists—

139

HOSPITALS AND PUBLIC HEALTH SERVICES, 1971

HOSPITALS

	Date of building and extensions	Total beds	Total full-time staff
Cape Breton County			
Sydney City	1918/53/68	200	430 (inc student nurses
St Rita's (Sydney)	1953/63	157	350 (inc student nurses)
General (Glace Bay)	1914/42/53	109	191
St Joseph (Glace Bay)	1939/62	140	192
New Waterford Consolidated	1963	88	187 (inc student nursing assistants)
St Elizabeth (North Sydney)	1954	146	244
Harbour View (Sydney Mines)	1908/18/50	84	118
Point Edward (TB Hospital)	1942	77	113
Cape Breton Mental (Sydney River)	1954	300	232
Inverness County			
St Mary's (Inverness)	1925	38	62
Inverness County Mem (Inverness)	1940	35	57
Sacred Heart (Chéticamp)	1938/58	38	60
Victoria County			
Buchanan Mem (Neil's Harbour)	1953	13	20
Victoria County Mem (Baddeck)	1949	23	28
Richmond County			
St Ann's Arichat	1854	22	28

Public Health Personnel

Cape Breton North Health Unit: North Sydney, Sydney Mines, Ingonish, Chéticamp, Margaree Forks, Baddeck

Cape Breton South Health Unit: Sydney, New Waterford, Glace Bay, St Peter's, Arichat, Port Hawkesbury, Port Hood

[Source: *Cape Breton Regional Health Services Study*, 1972]

Page 141 The aftermath of the wreck of the oiltanker, *Arrow*, 4 February 1970: (*above*) oil-fouled beaches at Arichat; (*below*) a 'slick-licker' cleaning up the mess around Chedabucto Bay

Page 142 Two of the leaders
of the Antigonish Movement:
(*left*) Father Moses Coady, in a
characteristic pose, addresses
the Co-operative Union of
Canada in Winnipeg, 1946;
(*below*) Father Jimmy
Tompkins in uncharacteristic
repose

one for every 5,351 residents compared to a national figure of
one per 2,500; there is no comprehensive rehabilitation facility;
the incidence of diabetes is 40 per cent higher than on mainland
Nova Scotia; influenza is 42 per cent higher and pneumonia
177 per cent higher; there is no special facility for treating res-
piratory diseases, other than the TB hospital at Point Edward,
or for other diseases; and there are no intensive-care units on
the island.

There was considerable concern by the medical profession and
citizens at the local level in industrial Cape Breton in the 1960s
about the lack of a diagnostic centre. In 1971–2, Cape Breton
tackled the health problem in the usual manner—they commissioned another study. In March 1972, the consultants (a
management firm) produced a three-volume report on *Cape
Breton Regional Health Services*. This suggested a shift away from
a hospital-based, illness-orientated system to one based on the
total health needs of the individual. The stress was laid on
regionalisation of health services with the aim of co-ordinating
all health resources on the island, providing the maximum level
of service at the community and regional level, developing a
pattern of service delivery 'to meet the needs of all consumers
of health services', and upgrading the existing facilities and
programmes. The basic unit of this system would not be the
hospital but the multipurpose health centre, which would
provide a broad range of medical, paramedical and social
services. The system would be run by a corporation.

During 1972, a variety of objections were raised to these
proposals. The doctors were worried that the formation of the
corporation would create a sort of medical 'Big Brother',
controlling them, and carrying out surveillance. To complicate
matters, the Nova Scotia Council of Health, an advisory board
to the Minister of Public Health, came out with a proposal that
divided the Province into seven regions and split Cape Breton in
two. Cape Breton County, all of Victoria County, the northern
part of Inverness County and most of Richmond County were

lumped together into one region, and the rest of Inverness County and a small part of Richmond County were part of a region that focussed on Antigonish.

The religious problem arose in Glace Bay where the study recommended closing one of the general hospitals. This would probably be the Glace Bay Hospital, which was built originally in 1914, and extended in 1942 and 1953. It is owned by a corporation, and abandoned mine shafts run under the property. St Joseph's Hospital has a main building erected in 1962, and is up-to-date. This hospital is owned and operated by the Roman Catholic Sisters of St Martha, who also own St Rita's Hospital in Sydney. Some fears were expressed by local people that the religious order would take over the medical services in Glace Bay. Indeed a caller to a local radio station in Sydney, in March 1972, claimed that the Sydney Community Health Council met on Sunday nights, in order to exclude Protestants from discussing the new health scheme. The caller explained that all good Protestants were in church on Sunday nights!

The health plan is supposed to unfold over a ten-year period. The wide range of physical environments and cultures pose a challenge to the main goal of the proposed health delivery system, with which no one on the island disagrees. This is to provide the best health services to Cape Bretoners, who have, for too long, been deprived of adequate medical care.

As a counterpart to attempts at change on the large scale, some Dutch Brothers are running a small therapeutic community at Mabou, in Inverness County. Here, at a former boys' school that looks out over a lovely vista of mountain and sea, brothers of the Order of Our Lady of the Seven Sorrows look after forty-five patients suffering from schizophrenia, senility and other mental illnesses. Some of the staff members are fluent in Gaelic, and the patients, who come from Inverness, Richmond, and Victoria Counties and still have the language, can converse in it. There are no fences or bars at St Mary's Hill; the patients move freely around the grounds and along nearby roads. And this somewhat isolated and remote part of Cape Breton provides an atmosphere of peace and quiet that is perhaps the best therapy for the mentally ill.

7   THE PEOPLE AND THEIR BELIEFS

FOR approximately one hundred and fifty years after their first contact with Europeans, the Micmac Indians played an active role in Cape Breton's history. They were regarded by the French as allies in their constant conflict with the British. They acted as guides and assisted in raids on settlements; on other occasions they were egged on by the French and made their own raids on New England settlements. Threats of Indian reprisals did much to keep the Acadians from pledging their allegiance to the British. Links with the French were strengthened by the work of missionaries like Father Maillard, who spent twenty-seven years ministering to the Micmacs. Two centuries later, he still holds a place of honour among them. The most important date in the Micmac calendar is in July, when the Indians gather for a three-day mission at Chapel Island, where Father Maillard preached his first sermon in 1735.

The Micmac language is in the Algonkian linguistic group. The Algonkian culture area stretches across Canada to Alberta and represents an adaptation to the central and eastern woodlands. Father Maillard completed a project, begun by an earlier missionary, Father LeClerq, of writing down the Micmac language in symbols. The system is a complicated one, and some anthropologists believe that its introduction delayed the teaching and writing of the language.

When Acadia passed into British hands, the status of the aboriginal inhabitants declined rapidly. At first they were neglected by the British, and their repeated requests for a

146

Catholic priest were ignored. Later, as Cape Breton was settled by immigrants, the Micmacs came to be regarded as a hindrance to the occupation of the country by newcomers. As early as 1812, settlers in the Red Islands area were petitioning the government to move the Indians so that a D. B. McNab could erect a mill.

The Micmacs called the Scottish settlers *saskatbaynit* ('flatheads') because of the flat bonnets they wore. As more and more of the good land was taken up, later settlers began to covet land reserved for the Indians. The Provincial government tried to protect the Indian land by legislation. In 1842, an act was passed 'To Provide for the Instruction and Permanent Settlement of the Indians', and the position of Commissioner of Indian Affairs was created. His job was to supervise and manage the Indian reserves, of which there were six on Cape Breton, totalling 12,205 acres. He was also to report on trespass, and on the sale and transfer of land. In 1845, the commissioner's report describes encroachment on the Indian lands by the Presbyterian Scots. In 1849, Commissioner Crawley reported that a settler named Chisholm had completely appropriated a small reserve at what is now Margaree Forks. In the Whycocomagh area, Scots settlers had not only removed timber from the Indian lands; they had also broken down fences to let their cattle graze, ruining hay and crops in the process. The commissioner laments:

> Under the present circumstances no adequate protection can be obtained for the Indian property. It would be in vain to seek a verdict from any jury in this Island against the trespassers on the reserves; nor perhaps would a member of the Bar be found willingly and effectually to advocate the cause of the Indians, inasmuch as he would thereby injure his own prospects, by damaging his own popularity.

In 1852, the title to all lands reserved for the Indians in Nova Scotia was vested in the Commissioner for Crown Lands. It became his job to protect the rights of Indians. With the coming of Confederation in 1867, the Indians became wards of the Federal government. Responsibility for them was shifted around among the various government departments; up to 1966, they were administered by the same department that looked after immigrants. In that year, a special Department of Indian Affairs and Northern Development was created.

The 1970 Band List (which contains the names of everyone the Federal government considers to be an Indian) enumerated 2,442 Indians on Cape Breton, living on five reserves. One of the reserves, Sydney (Membertou) is located in an urban area. The other four—Eskasoni, Whycocomagh, Middle River (Nyanza) and Chapel Island (Barra Head)—are all in rural areas.

In Cape Breton, as elsewhere in Canada, there is growing militancy among the Indians. In 1969, the Union of Nova Scotia Indians was organised with the slogan 'United we stand, Divided we fall'. The union attempts to promote the rights, welfare and progress of all Indians in Nova Scotia, from its headquarters in Sydney. The union publishes a monthly newspaper, the *Micmac News* which has a wide distribution in Nova Scotia and New Brunswick. In March 1972, the Nova Scotia Native Women's Association was formed 'to improve the living and working conditions of native women throughout Nova Scotia'.

Among Cape Breton Micmacs, a favourite method of signing off a letter is 'yours in recognition of aboriginal rights'. Aboriginal rights is probably the major concern of Canadian Indians at this time. Aboriginal rights involve the recognition that the traditional peoples of Canada 'owned' the land before the white men came—or at least took freely of the fruits of it. When the white men came, they took the land in some cases, dispossessing the Indians, and ruined traditional hunting and trapping areas. In some parts of Canada, the government signed treaties with the Indians, who accepted the rule of the government, and received certain benefits in return. No treaties were signed between the Micmacs of Nova Scotia and the government of Canada. In 1972, the Federal government still did not recognise aboriginal rights, but it was negotiating with Indian groups in an attempt to work out a fair deal for the Indians. There are at least two aspects to Indian rights that are of overwhelming importance. One involves a recognition by the government of Canada of the validity of the Indian way of life, and the other is the settlement by cash of claims for using—or ruining—parts of Canada that the Indians once occupied. Many Indians in Canada seek a cash settlement—payment for the land, compensation for lost resources, and money to extinguish all future claims, so that no Indian will come back to the government and claim that he has been defrauded of his aboriginal rights. The Micmacs are seeking a settlement that will provide them with certain services—sewers, street lighting, police protection—and also exemption from such taxes as the 7 per cent Provincial sales tax which pays for part of Medicare and hospital care for provincial residents.

While working outwards, and making demands on the larger society, the Micmacs are also trying hard to solve their own problems—bad housing, low educational levels, lack of marketable skills, juvenile delinquency, and alcoholism. They face an additional problem of discrimination, which cannot be legislated against. It is based on an attitude of mind on the part of some Cape Bretoners that downgrades the worth of the Indian and his culture, and implies that what he has to offer society is somehow inferior. Until this attitude is eradicated, improving the status of the Indian will be uphill work.

THE ACADIANS

The Indians had their lands taken away from them; the Acadians were taken away from their lands. When Britain took control of the mainland of Nova Scotia, in accordance with the

149

terms of the Treaty of Utrecht in 1713, the Acadian inhabitants were given the choice of moving to French territory or remaining—as subjects of the British crown. Most chose to remain; but from mistrust of the British and fear of the French and their Indian allies, the Acadians refused to take the required oath of allegiance. They maintained their refusal for forty years and for forty years the British avoided facing the alternative of removing them. In the shadow of the final struggle for survival between the French and British empires in North America, the decision to deport the Acadians was inevitable. However, its inevitability could hardly excuse the callous manner in which Governor Lawrence carried out the deportation. Instead of the Acadians being sent to France or French territory, they were distributed among the British American colonies; they were not allowed to take anything with them, and members of the same family were in many cases sent to different destinations. Some evaded the round-up and hid out in the forest; others made their way to Quebec or Louisiana. With the British conquest and the coming of peace in 1763, the presence of Acadians in British territory no longer posed a potential threat. Those who had remained came out of hiding and others returned from exile. Many of these found their way to Cape Breton, where they settled in what are now Richmond and Inverness Counties.

Expulsion had turned the Acadians who survived into a tough and resilient group, with a strong determination to preserve their own identity. Their descendants have retained this determination to go their own way, rather than to merge with the French-speaking people of Quebec. Today, the only county in the whole of Nova Scotia with an Acadian majority is Richmond County, which includes the picturesque Isle Madame, where Acadian communities such as Arichat, Petit-de-Grat, and D'Escousse are located. The 1961 census shows that 6,669 out of a total county population of 11,374 were of French origin; these people would be almost entirely Acadians.

In Inverness County, there were 4,891 people of French origin. The rest of the 25,070 Acadians live and work in the industrial area of Cape Breton County.

Among Acadian historians and sociologists, it is generally agreed that the community in Canada where the Acadian tradition is best preserved today is Chéticamp in northern Inverness County. This community was established in 1790 by Acadians returning from exile in St Pierre and Miquelon. Among the first settlers, there were the Chiassons, the Deveaus and the Aucoins. Today, in the Chéticamp phone listing, these names still dominate; in 1972 there were 112 Aucoins, seventy-two Deveaus (in various spellings) and sixty-nine Chiassons.

The French spoken by the Chéticantins and other Acadians differs from that spoken in Quebec and France. It has many of the characteristics of mid-seventeenth-century French and of the kind of provincial patois spoken in the west of France. For example, *je* is used rather than *nous* for 'we': *je chantons* (we sing); *je mangerons* (we shall eat); where *o* is followed by *n* or *m* it becomes *ou* as in *poume* (apple) instead of *pomme* and *houme* (man) instead of *homme*. Only in Chéticamp will you hear someone use *se gréer* (literally 'to rig a ship') instead of *se vêtir* for dressing oneself. At least one word coined by the Acadians has passed into ordinary usage in Cape Breton. *Barachois* is used to describe a lagoon or pond cut off from a larger body of water by a neck of land or a sand bar.

Chéticamp, like most homogenous Acadian communities, focuses on the church. The present church was built and finished under Father Fiset, who was parish priest between 1875 and 1909. Father Fiset was an extraordinary man, dynamic and very much concerned with the material as well as the spiritual welfare of his parishioners. In 1896, he purchased the lobster factory from the Jersey firm of Robin because he did not think they were giving the Chéticantins a fair deal. In 1907, he set up the Great Northern Mining Company to exploit a mountain of gypsum which a prospector had brought to his attention. The mine closed down in 1913 and, as usual, the Chéticantins wrote a satirical song about the event.

The Acadian scholar, Father Anselme Chiasson, writing of the Acadian character, has this to say:

> The Acadian carries in his soul the traces of past sufferings. His ancestors lived for a long time dispossessed, hunted down and dishonoured. The earliest pages of his history were written in his blood; he still carries the mark. Brutally uprooted from his land he has now turned to the sea . . . For a long period in their history, the Acadians lived in isolation. On the whole this has tended to hold back their development and to make them feel inferior . . . Having suffered, the Acadian is kind to others, understanding, sympathetic, sensitive, compassionate and hospitable.

Chéticamp's isolation ended with the construction of the Cabot Trail, and the establishment of the Cape Breton Highlands National Park. More and more young Acadians are learning and speaking English, but the old traditions still survive and are likely to do so for a long time to come.

THE SCOTS

As immigrants, the Scots were comparative late-comers, but they arrived in sufficient numbers to impress their character and culture on the island. It has become commonplace in Cape Breton to remark how much the physical landscape resembles that of Scotland; the Lakes O'Law and the Three Sisters are like parts of the Trossachs, and sections of the upland plateau in the north have the same harsh, rugged look of much of the Scottish Highlands. But physical resemblances are not restricted to landscapes. A Cape Bretoner recalls visiting Barra, the island from which the ancestors of the people in his community came. He was surprised to see what a strong resemblance there was between the Barra people and those in his home community, three or four generations removed. His surprise turned to astonishment when he came face to face with the double of a friend whose funeral he had recently attended.

Because many of the early immigrants arrived in groups and settled down together to form communities, their speech has not changed much. People whose ancestors came from Harris, Lewis, Barra, and North and South Uist still speak the Gaelic very much as it is spoken in their ancestral communities. Even when conversing in English, many of these Gaelic speakers can be identified geographically. It is the survival of the Gaelic language as much as anything else that ranks Cape Breton as an outpost of Scottish Highland culture. Indeed, for the purposes of the 100,000-word 'Historical Dictionary of Scottish Gaelic', being compiled by the Celtic Department of Glasgow University, Cape Breton is considered an off-island of Scotland.

The Gaelic language flourished where there were few English-speaking settlers, and the island even had a completely Gaelic newspaper. Jonathan G. MacKinnon published the first issue of his four-page weekly Gaelic newspaper on 28 May 1892. Called *Mac-Talla* (Echo), it was financed by public subscription and was the first Gaelic newspaper anywhere to carry advertising. In the following year, four more pages were added, and by its third year of existence, *Mac-Talla*'s subscription list had grown to 1,100. The number of subscribers never exceeded 1,400, and many of these neglected to pay. By 1901, the paper was appearing every other week, and finally, on 24 June 1904, *Mac-Talla* was published for the last time.

Figures on the number of Gaelic speakers in Cape Breton have always been, at best, broad approximations. Census figures indicate only those reporting Gaelic as their 'mother tongue' and do not include those whose first language is English, but who also 'have the Gaelic'. In 1890, in a speech to the Canadian House of Commons, on his motion to make Gaelic an official language, T. R. McInnes claimed that in Cape Breton 'of the 100,000 of the population, I think I am within the mark when I say that at least three-fourths speak the Gaelic language'. By the 1940s, this number had dropped to about 35,000, and in the 1961 census, only 3,352 people reported

Gaelic as their mother tongue. In 1971, a visiting Gaelic linguist from Scotland interviewed one hundred Gaelic speakers in Cape Breton, and calculated that there were altogether 1,500 of them on the island. The Gaelic Society of Cape Breton gives a figure of 5,000, and the exact number is probably somewhere in between.

The decline of the language was speeded up by teachers who punished pupils for speaking it, and by parents who discouraged their children from 'wasting time' on Gaelic. Some attempts in the past were made to halt the decline. In 1921, the Provincial Department of Education allowed the teaching of the language as part of a school curriculum, provided enough of the students wanted to learn it and the trustees could provide a qualified Gaelic teacher. In 1950, the department went a step further and appointed Major C. I. N. MacLeod as Gaelic Advisor in the adult education division. However, when Major MacLeod left in 1958 to head the Department of Celtic Studies at St Francis Xavier University, the position was allowed to lapse. In 1939, a Gaelic college was opened at St Ann's, where Norman McLeod and his followers had flourished a century before. The founder of the college, Rev A. W. R. MacKenzie, wanted to encourage not only the teaching of the Gaelic, but also to revive the traditional highland crafts such as the weaving of tartans. His hope was for a sheep on every hill, and a loom in every house. Today the college operates a summer school, where young people from Cape Breton and elsewhere learn piping, drumming, and highland dancing, as well as Gaelic.

In 1972, three events indicated that there was a revival of interest in Gaelic and a concern for its continuing existence as a dynamic facet of Cape Breton life. In April, for the first time in twenty-five years, a play in Gaelic was performed. *Tha Katie Ann a Tighnin Dhachaidh* (*Katie is Coming Home*), attended by more than 300 people, was a satire written by the Rev Stanley Macdonald, and concerns the visit made to her home in Cape Breton by a young lady who has acquired a Boston accent and claims to have forgotten the Gaelic. Her family continues to speak to her only in Gaelic and eventually she drops her airs and joins the conversation in her native language.

In May, the Provincial Department of Education announced that it would share in the cost of teaching Gaelic in Cape Breton schools, providing that sufficient interest was shown. Starting with the 1972–3 school year, two peripatetic qualified teachers will give Gaelic classes in six schools in Inverness County: Inverness, Judique, Mabou, Margaree Forks, Port Hood, and Whycocomagh.

In July, the Gaelic Society of Cape Breton, founded in 1969 to encourage the preservation of Gaelic culture, received a Federal government grant of $6,000 (£2,400) to help in presenting a three-week *Caidreach nan Gaidheal* (Gaelic gathering) in Sydney. In announcing their project, the society described it as a sharing with the community at large of the Gaelic culture and traditions as well as an attempt to open communications between the older and younger generations of Cape Breton Gaels. The three-week 'folk school' featured, in addition to instruction in the Gaelic language, films, lectures and seminars on various aspects of Scottish Gaelic culture. It concluded with a large-scale ceilidh at the local arena, featuring piping, dancing and singing.

Music was an essential part of the highlander's culture, and did much to relieve the drudgery of settling in the new land. One popular entertainment was the composing of songs about people. These songs could be satirical, insulting or complimentary, depending on the temperament of the local bard. It is a tradition that still exists, as the visiting Gaelic linguist discovered. He had set off on a word-collecting expedition to Cape North, and stopped on the way to raise the hood of his borrowed convertible car. While he was struggling to get the top up, he was attacked by a horde of mosquitoes, and after cursing them in Gaelic, he returned to Sydney. Word got around and at a ceilidh a few days later, he found himself recording a Gaelic song about his battle with the insects.

Many of the songs and melodies for the pipes and the fiddle have been passed down through generations from the settlers who brought them from their homeland. A professor from St Francis Xavier University recalls a visit she made to Eigg, the Scottish island from which her mother's people had come. One evening, the crofter with whom she was boarding took down his fiddle, and the first tune he played was the one with which her own mother had always begun her selection.

Singers, pipers, Cape Breton fiddlers, step-dancers and highland dancers all perform annually at a popular form of Cape Breton entertainment—open-air Scottish concerts. These are held throughout the summer at Big Pond, Broad Cove, Frenchvale, Glendale, Johnstown, and Mabou. These provide ample evidence that the highlander's musical tradition is very much alive.

In 1956, a site was chosen at Hector's Point, just outside Iona, for a highland village, to provide a visual record of the pioneer life of the Scots who had come to Cape Breton. Sixteen years later, due to shortage of funds and organisational problems, only the museum had been completed. This houses an interesting collection of pioneer relics and artifacts, labelled in Gaelic and English. In 1973 work began on building a village, representing three stages of Scottish settlement—the 'black houses' the pioneers left behind, the log buildings of the first settlers, and the frame houses which replaced them. When completed it will give Cape Breton Scots a glimpse into their own past.

OTHER INCOMERS

There were other French-speaking settlers on Cape Breton besides the Acadians. French Huguenots from the Island of Jersey dominated the fishing trade on the island after Louisbourg fell. A distinguished Cape Bretoner of Jersey ancestry was the constitutional expert, Sir John Bourinot, whose handbook, *Practice and Procedure of Parliament*, published in 1884, is still in use as an authoritative source today.

The United Empire Loyalists helped to found Sydney. Many were professional men in the former colonies, and some brought slaves with them. Other slaves came to Cape Breton on the outbreak of the War of 1812, when freedom was promised to any slave who escaped from his American master and joined the British. A few of these refugees found their way to Whycocomagh, a settlement of Gaelic speakers. It was perhaps one of their descendants whom Kipling took as his model for the cook in *Captains Courageous*, the 'coal black Celt with the second sight' who came from 'the innards of Cape Breton', and spoke Gaelic.

At the beginning of the twentieth century, immigrants poured into industrial Cape Breton to work in the coal mines and the steel mills. They came from Russia, Poland, Hungary, Italy, Germany and the Ukraine. One of the first to arrive was a Ukrainian, Nicolas Fedora, in 1901. When other Ukrainians and Poles came to work in the steel plant, the company hired Fedora as an interpreter and his home became the focus of the Ukrainian community.

During World War I, West Indians who could no longer get to Britain arrived in the Maritimes. They came mainly from Jamaica, British Guiana, Bermuda and St Vincent and many of them settled in Sydney. Just outside Whitney Pier, under the shadow of the Victoria Road Bridge, is a building with the incongruous sign on it 'West Indian Cricket Club'. It is actually a social club. A number of Lebanese also established themselves in Sydney, where at one time they all lived along the same street. A number of Cape Bretoners of Lebanese origin are prominent business and professional men.

Each new group of incomers added to the island's human diversity and complexity. Like the Acadians and the Scots, people of the same ethnic origin tended to settle together, and in the industrial landscape there is at least one small group of houses that looks as if it had been transported from Eastern Europe. One of the binding ties between the different minority groups was their religion, and the priests and clergymen played a significant role in the development of the island and its people.

RELIGION

The island's churches dominate the landscape, with their white wooden walls and black roofs. Some, like the Catholic church at Mabou, have tall, graceful spires, while others, like the Presbyterian church at Albert Bridge, have square towers. A few are built of stone. St Peter's in Chéticamp is visible for miles, its roof and tower shining in the sun, and the church at Boisdale is faintly reminiscent of the abbey at Iona in Scotland.

There is a church tradition that Cape Breton was the first place on the North American continent where holy communion was celebrated. It is said that Sir Humphrey Gilbert, half brother of Sir Walter Ralegh, landed on the shores of Cape Breton while leading an expedition in 1578, and that the chaplain of the expedition, one Master Wolfall, celebrated holy communion somewhere on the island.

In 1629, the first Jesuits, Father de Vieuxport and Father Vimont, arrived in St Ann's Bay. A chapel was built and dedicated to St Ann, who was later adopted by the Indians as their patroness, and in 1634 a mission was officially founded. This closed in 1641, and the Jesuits never returned to the island. In St Peter's three Capuchin Fathers established a mission that lasted from 1645 to 1655. There is no further record of the presence of priests on the island until the founding of Louisbourg. It was the Recollet Fathers who ministered to the needs of the French inhabitants, while the Seminary of Foreign Missions in Paris sent out priests to attend to the Indians. There were no resident priests or ministers on Cape Breton for nearly twenty-eight years following the fall of Louisbourg.

Page 159   Traditional crafts and activities: (*above*) a performance of the sword-dance at the annual Highland Village Day in Iona; (*below*) hooked rugs, of beautiful workmanship and subtlety of colour, are an Acadian speciality

Page 160   Tourism: (*above*) Baddeck, a favourite tourist resort and a major yachting centre on the island; (*below*) a kite frozen in stone and glass—the Alexander Graham Bell Museum in Baddeck

Roman Catholics

The first permanent Catholic parish in Cape Breton was established in Arichat in 1786. With the arrival of emigrants from Scotland the number of Catholics on the island increased rapidly. In 1818, the first parish of Catholic highlanders was founded at Judique. By 1861, when the census listed 33,386 Catholics out of a total population of 63,083, there were twenty-two parishes with resident priests and seven native Cape Bretoners had become priests.

Cape Breton was part of the Diocese of Quebec until 1829, when the island was joined ecclesiastically to Nova Scotia. The bishop of the diocese was Bishop William Fraser. In 1844, as a result of numerous complaints that were received about him, the Vatican sent out a clerical counsultor to investigate. He found that the trouble arose from the conflict between the Scots and the Irish, and reported:

> Furthermore, neither group likes to be ruled by a prelate who is not of the same nation or at least sprung from it; the Irish are inclined to complain should the bishop be a Scot, and the Scots if he be Irish . . . The present bishop, Monsignor Fraser, is a native of Scotland and hence inclined to have greater regard for his fellow Scot than for the Irish.

The problem was solved when the diocese was divided into two and Bishop Fraser took over the part containing most of the Scots, namely Cape Breton Island and the eastern part of the mainland of Nova Scotia. In 1886, the diocese was renamed the Diocese of Antigonish, and it is here that the Cathedral and the Bishop's 'Palace' are located today.

The Catholics are still the most numerous single denomination. The 1961 census reports 104,575 Roman Catholics out of a total population of 169,865. In 1972, there were sixty-nine parishes on the island.

Presbyterians

The first Presbyterian minister to visit Cape Breton was Dr James McGregor of Pictou, on the mainland of Nova Scotia. He came in 1798 at the request of the Sutherlands, a family of Presbyterians who lived south of Sydney. Dr McGregor and his party travelled by open boat to St Peter's, and then across the Bras d'Or Lakes. At the head of East Bay the party started to walk the twelve miles or so that separated them from their destination, but they got hopelessly lost in the woods. They retrieved their boat, sailed back down East Bay, through Barra Strait, and up St Andrew's Channel to their destination, a distance of eighty miles. Despite the hazards of travelling in Cape Breton, Dr McGregor made a second trip to the island in 1818.

Presbyterians date the beginnings of their church from 20 May 1820, when Norman McLeod and his followers settled at St Ann's and built the first Presbyterian church in Cape Breton.

The next Presbyterian minister to found a congregation was the Rev William Miller, who settled at Mabou in 1822. Like James McGregor, Norman McLeod and other early Presbyterian ministers in Nova Scotia, Miller was a secessionist from the established Church of Scotland. Two years after his arrival he built a church. His ministry was not an easy one, since he was a Lowland Scot without the Gaelic, but he remained minister at Mabou until his death in 1861. Alexander Farquharson, the first minister of the established Church of Scotland to be sent to Cape Breton, arrived in 1833 and made his headquarters in Middle River. By the end of his first year he had preached in nearly every Presbyterian community on the island. One of the most colourful ministers was the Rev Peter McLean, who settled in Whycocomagh and preached with such evangelical fervour that people came from miles around to hear him. Not surprisingly, Norman McLeod did not approve of such emotionalism and referred to McLean as the 'ranting revivalist'. McLean left for Scotland in 1842, but returned for a visit in 1853, when he conducted a communion service which aroused such a response in the nearly five thousand people present that it was spoken of for years after.

In 1875, the different groups of Presbyterians united to form the Presbyterian Church of Canada, but less than fifty years later there was disagreement over a vital point: whether or not the Presbyterian Church of Canada should join with the Methodists and Congregationalists to form the United Church of Canada. Feelings ran high; congregations were split on the issue. In many families brother and sister, parent and child, and husband and wife were locked in bitter conflict over whether they should remain Presbyterians or merge their religious identity into that of the United Church. The final vote of the General Assembly of the Presbyterian Church was for merger, and in 1925, when the act creating the United Church of Canada was passed, nearly 70 per cent of the Presbyterians in Canada joined the newly formed church. The remainder chose to stay within a re-organised Presbyterian Church of Canada.

The responses in Cape Breton varied. In Sydney, for example, the majority of the members of all three churches, St Andrew's, Falmouth and St James, decided to join the United Church, while the dissenting minorities of each congregation united to form the Bethal Presbyterian and built a new church. In Catalone, Whycocomagh and Baddeck the Presbyterian churches were transformed into the United churches, and the minorities established new ones. In other communities the Presbyterian congregations remained as they were.

There are thirty Presbyterian congregations on the island today, and the 1961 census for Cape Breton lists 11,858 Presbyterians. In 1968, the Evangelical United Brethren also became part of the United Church of Canada. There are 40,965 United Church members in Cape Breton.

Anglicans

The Anglican churches in Cape Breton are part of the Anglican Diocese of Nova Scotia, the oldest of the colonial bishoprics. Over 90 per cent of Cape Breton's 15,779 Anglicans live in Cape Breton County, mostly in and around Sydney. St George's was the first Anglican parish to be established. It dates from 1 June 1786 when the parish minister, Ranna Cositt, of New England, took up his appointment. Work on the construction of a church began soon after his arrival. The present St George's church retains only the foundations of the original structure. The parish was limited to the township of Sydney and was later joined by two more, Christ Church and St Albans. In 1828 a new parish was established at Arichat, and other parishes subsequently came into existence.

Other denominations

Most of the 3,005 Baptists listed in the 1961 census live in Cape Breton County. The earliest Baptist church was Calvary Baptist Church built at North Sydney in 1825.

The Holy Ghost Ukrainian Catholic Church in Sydney, with its characteristic onion-shaped spires, was built by the Ukrainian community in 1912. Nearly all Cape Breton's 588 Ukrainian Catholics live in the Whitney Pier area of Sydney.

Also in Whitney Pier is the only parish in Canada of the African Orthodox Church, an offshoot of Methodism. St Phillip's was established in 1921 by the Rev William Ernest Robertson.

There are three synagogues. The oldest congregation is the Congregation Sons of Israel, incorporated in Glace Bay in 1901. There are two congregations in Sydney: The Sons of Israel Temple and the Hebrew Congregation of Whitney Pier.

THE PEOPLE AND THEIR BELIEFS

The early settlers brought their superstitions with them. An indication of just how deeply rooted these were, is given in a report from a Mr Crawley to the Provincial government in 1834. Following the wreck of the *Astraea*, when only three out of 251 people aboard escaped, and many bodies were washed ashore, Crawley asked for some remuneration for the local inhabitants who, although only poor fishermen, attended to the burial of the victims. He says, 'They were also exceedingly careful that everyone should be duly interred before sunset, being persuaded that the inhabitants would be nightly visited by the spirits of such as remained above ground'.

Story-telling by expert narrators was a favourite pastime of both the Scots and Acadians. The Scottish narrators, especially, drew on the supernatural as material for their stories.

Witchcraft and second-sight

Among the Acadians of Chéticamp there was the firm belief that many of the Jerseymen, who controlled the fish trade and to a certain extent the lives of the Chéticantins, were witches. In his *Chéticamp: Historie et Traditions acadiennes*, Father Chiasson tells of a famous case that has become embellished and exaggerated by many repetitions, and concerns the popular priest, Father Fiset.

The servant of a parishioner had a hex put on her by a Jerseyman called Charles Romril. When Father Fiset tried to exorcise the girl, the spell was transferred to him, or to be more precise, to his rectory. Noise and chaos reigned, and when one of the rooms burst into flames another parishioner vowed he would do something about it. He built a snowman and then, taking his gun, he approached the figure by going forward three paces and back two. When he was at a certain distance, he put a bullet through the side of the snowman. At that moment, Romril developed a pain in his side and, as the snowman

165

melted, the pain increased. When the snowman had melted away completely, Romril died.

With so many inhabitants of Celtic ancestry, it is not surprising to read and hear of those who have second-sight. In Cape Breton this is called double-sight, probably because the Gaelic word, *da-shealladh* means literally 'two sights'. The double-sighted individual sometimes receives a glimpse of coming events, usually the death of someone close to him or her. The commonest manifestation of this precognition seems to be a knocking on a door or wall, heard when there is no one around who could have caused it. The knocks, usually three, foretell a death. In a case recounted to the authors, the death that followed the hearing of three firm knocks was that of the informants' grandfather. Another type of manifestation, described by Helen Creighton in *Bluenose Ghosts* and by Mary Fraser in *Folklore of Nova Scotia*, is the witnessing of some aspect of a funeral: hearing a coffin being made; seeing the body laid out, or witnessing a funeral procession. Mary Fraser remarks, 'Very few Nova Scotia Celts are brave enough to walk in the centre of the highway after nightfall, for fear of encountering any of these phantom funeral processions'. She was writing in the early 1930s. In Cape Breton today, the Celt who walked in the centre of the highway after dark would soon find himself the reason for, rather than the observer of, a funeral procession.

However, the most famous supernatural happening in Cape Breton occurred before the arrival of the Scottish immigrants. It took place in Sydney Barracks while DesBarres was lieutenant-governor, and involved an apparition seen by two young officers of the 33rd Regiment.

Captain John Coape Sherbrooke (later lieutenant-governor of Nova Scotia) and Lieutenant George Wynyard were reading in Wynyard's quarters around 4 pm on the afternoon of 15 October 1785. The room in which they sat had a door opening into the corridor and another into Wynyard's bedroom. There was one window in the bedroom, but it had been sealed up for the winter. Sherbrooke happened to look up, and saw a young man, pale and lightly clad, standing in the doorway that led to the corridor. On calling Wynyard's attention to him, he was surprised to see his friend go deathly pale. As they watched, the intruder slowly crossed the room in which they sat and passed into the bedroom, at which point Wynyard exclaimed that it was his brother. Both men rushed into the bedroom, only to find it empty! They called in another officer Lieutenant Ralph Gore, to help in the search, but no trace of the mysterious figure could be found. Gore recommended that they keep quiet about the event. However, Wynyard, upset and convinced that his brother must be dead, spoke of his fears to others. Soon the story was out, and when the governor of Nova Scotia heard about it he sent a group of civilians to investigate. Because relations between Lt-Col Yorke, the military commander, and DesBarres were strained, Yorke refused the civilian investigators permission to interview the parties concerned. In June, with the arrival of the first mails, Wynyard learned of the death of his brother in India at approximately the same time that the apparition had appeared.

Over the years, the 'Wynyard Ghost Story' has been much quoted. Sir Walter Scott, writing of it in his *Letters on Demonology and Witchcraft*, complained that 'although all agree in the general event, scarcely two, even those who pretend to the best information, tell the story in the same way'. When Helen Creighton was collecting accounts of supernatural experiences for her *Bluenose Ghosts*, she was given another version. In this one the scene was set in Sydney Barracks but the time was around 1873, and the apparition was that of an officer stationed in Sydney who, while visiting England, was taken ill and died there. His ghost was seen by a group of his fellow officers. Dr Creighton's informant assured her that her father, who had told her the story, had it first-hand from the officers involved.

A folk hero

Angus MacAskill 'the gentle giant' was the folk hero of all Cape Bretoners. He was born in Harris in Scotland in 1825, and his parents moved to Englishtown and settled there. At fourteen, Angus was known as St Ann's Big Boy or *Gille Mor*. Eventually he grew to 7ft 9in in height, and to weigh 425lb. He earned his living fishing and soon became famous for feats of strength. He seems to have been a kind and gentle man who was occasionally goaded to fury by people who tried to provoke him because he was 'different'. An American fishing captain who weighed 300lb was thrown over a 10ft woodpile when he taunted MacAskill. When the giant was about nineteen, he went on tour. There seem to be some doubts about his real height at this time, which was given as 7ft 7in, 7ft 2in, and 7ft 3½in. But he was big and he was strong, and he travelled through Newfoundland, the USA, and the West Indies, even to Cuba, where he was known as 'Mount KasKill'. It was alleged that he was taunted by some French sailors either in New York or New Orleans, and lifted an anchor weighing either 2,200lb or 2,700lb. One of the flukes caught in his shoulder and crippled him. Angus MacAskill returned home in the mid-1850s, and settled down in Englishtown. He built a store and bought a grist mill and lived out the rest of his days in ease and prosperity. Giant MacAskill died of 'brain fever' on 8 August 1863, aged thirty-eight. He lies buried in the country churchyard at Englishtown. His original tombstone described him as 'A dutiful son, a kind brother, just in all dealings, Universally respected by all his acquaintances'. This tombstone is now in the Pioneer Museum at St Ann's. Over his grave now is a marble tombstone on which the date of his death is given as 6 August. Inaccuracy has a way of dogging folk heroes, even to the grave.

Treasure

Mabou, the coast opposite Margaree (or Sea Wolf) Island, Ingonish, and Cow Bay are all reputed to have been at one time or another the site of pirate treasure. The tradition for the digging up of buried treasure specifies that under no circumstances must the digger speak. Even if, as in the case of the digger at Ingonish, a sword dangling by a thread appears over his head, he must remain silent. At the utterance of the first syllable, the treasure will vanish and not reappear for seven years. Perhaps the phantom ship that appears in the night from time to time opposite Port Hood was once a pirate ship. Before the eyes of the startled observer, the ship, fully rigged, burns down to the hull and drifts slowly off into the night.

Not all the legends involve treasure buried by pirates. The fabled treasure of Louisbourg is supposed to have been smuggled out and buried. One story has a young priest smuggling out the church plate just before the fortress was captured and burying it near the beach in Ingonish. Many years later he returned and dug it up. Chests of treasure are also reputed to have been smuggled out of Louisbourg, but in the process the bridge leading from the pond to the harbour dock collapsed and the chests sank deep into the mud. Several attempts were made over the years to recover them, but without success.

The most famous of Cape Breton's treasures is that of the pay-ship *Le Chameau* which sank off Louisbourg in August 1725. This treasure led to a court case in Canada in the 1960s. *Le Chameau* of 600 tons, carried a hundred crew and 216 passengers. It also carried 82,010 livres in gold and silver coins, the pay for the troops in Quebec. *Le Chameau* was caught in an east-south-east gale near Cape Breton, and crashed on a reef 4,000ft off shore. All on board were drowned. It took Alex Storm, a stubborn Dutch-Canadian, a great deal of effort to locate and recover *Le Chameau*'s treasure. In July 1961, he recovered one cannon, two brass cannon breeches, a small bronze ring, and a silver livre embossed with the head of Louis XV and dated 1724. He entered into a partnership with four other men to continue searching for the treasure. During his underwater forays, Storm was nibbled by ocean perch, stung by blue jellyfish, and driven out of the water by six curious sharks. In 1965, he formed a new team with Harvey MacLeod, a Louisbourg marine mechanic, and David MacEachern, another diving enthusiast who was a surveyor at Fortress Louisbourg. Storm secured a licence under the Treasure Trove Act, and the three men agreed to use every weekend and holiday to look for the *Chameau* treasure. They collected more information on the ship from the Director of the Naval Museum in Paris, and obtained the original drawings made during the first search for *Le Chameau* in 1726. Using Little Lorraine as a base, the group set out old quart beer bottles as markers over the area where the ship was lost, and began an intensive search. An underwater tow made out of an old bedstead caused a great deal of derision among the local people, but it proved to be the key to the success of the venture. On Sunday, 19 September 1965, after many delays and difficulties, Storm noted a cannon on the sea floor, then a mass of coins, and, of all things, a pocket watch. On the following Wednesday, they dived again and began to gather more coins. These had become wedged in a crevice in the rocks, and were of gold. For a number of weeks until their last dive on 18 October, the divers picked gold and silver coins off the bottom.

Storm kept the coins under his bed until late in November when they were stored in a bank on Charlotte Street in Sydney. The value of the treasure was estimated at $700,000 (£280,000). The May 1966 edition of *Argosy* magazine carried the full story for the first time, and the three men became the focus of worldwide publicity. But the happy ending to the story of Alex Storm's tenacity and courage was marred. In April 1966, his four original partners filed an injunction restraining him from selling the treasure on the grounds that part of it belonged to them. While the *Chameau* treasure was being cleaned and prepared for sale, a series of court cases dragged on in Halifax. Finally the Supreme Court of Canada ruled unanimously that the four men were entitled to a 25 per cent share. In December 1971, 705 items from *Le Chameau* were auctioned in New York, and realised $199,680 (£79,872). An emerald ring went for $4,750 (£1,900), and a single gold coin, minted in Dijon in 1724, fetched $1,100 (£440). Alex Storm still lives in Louisbourg and has continued his hunt for treasure around the coasts of Cape Breton. He has recovered Spanish pieces-of-eight; French, Dutch and English coins from the British warship *Feversham*, which sank in 1711; and cannon and other artifacts from the *Colombo*, which sank in 1828.

8   THE VISITOR'S ISLAND

THERE is plenty for the visitor to see and do on Cape Breton, but there are also numerous quiet spots, many solitary trails, and acres of emptiness accessible by car and bus, on foot or by canoe.

Cape Breton can be reached by air, rail, road and sea. Sydney Airport is located just off the main Sydney to Glace Bay Highway. There are daily Air Canada flights between Sydney and Boston, Deer Lake (Newfoundland), Fredericton, Gander, Halifax, Moncton, Montreal, New York (John F. Kennedy Airport), Ottawa, St John, St John's, Stephenville, Toronto and Yarmouth. Halifax is only forty minutes away by air, and it takes about four hours to fly from Sydney to Boston. Sydney is also served by a regional carrier, Eastern Provincial Airways. Two flights a day connect Sydney with Charlottetown, the capital of Prince Edward Island, and St John's, the capital of Newfoundland. The flight to Charlottetown continues on to Montreal. Air St Pierre flies daily to St Pierre and Miquelon, the two French islands south of Newfoundland; the flights take an hour.

Canadian National operates all trains on Cape Breton; the railway slices through the centre of the island, linking Port Hawkesbury and Sydney. Truro is the main railway junction for Nova Scotia; here the trains are routed west to Montreal, east to Sydney, or south to Halifax. There are only 'two up

172

and two down' trains each day. One is a Railiner which stops on signal at most places along the line, with scheduled stops at North Sydney, Sydney Mines and Port Hawkesbury. The 'fast train' also stops at North Sydney with signal stops at Sydney Mines and Orangedale. This train, the Scotian, is a through train from Montreal, equipped with sleeping cars, a restaurant and bar, and a snack bar. The railway station at Sydney is near the Central Business District, but the North Sydney station is about a mile away from Newfoundland ferry dock, and a taxi is required to get from the train to the boat. North Sydney is fifteen miles from Sydney, and the journey takes about half an hour. The railway comes into Sydney at grade, and crosses about six roads in the built-up area before it reaches the station.

Canadian National also operates the ferry system. There is a large parking lot at the North Sydney ferry dock, and the terminal building contains a snack bar, ticket offices, and an information booth for both Nova Scotia and Newfoundland. There is a ferry service four times a day (five trips on Saturday and Sunday) during the summer, and twice a day out of season, between North Sydney and Port aux Basques. The crossing takes about seven hours. Advance booking is required for passengers and cars on the night runs. Tickets have to be claimed and reservations confirmed two hours before departure. There is also a service three times weekly between North Sydney and Argentia, which is just eighty miles south of St John's. This route takes eighteen hours and reservations are required. The ferries are large, modern and air-conditioned, and the fares reasonable.

The bus service to and from the island also consists of 'two up and two down'. The Acadian bus service is fast and punctual, and the drivers are pleasant and helpful. The bus drives right to the ferry parking lot in North Sydney, which lies at the end of the Cape Breton section of the TransCanada Highway. The trips originate in Halifax, Nova Scotia. In 1972, one bus left there at 2 pm and went via Port Hawkesbury, through Baddeck, and then along the TransCanada Highway to North Sydney and Sydney, arriving there at 10.20 pm. The morning bus left Halifax at 8.15 am and went through Port Hawkesbury and then by way of the southern route through St Peter's and along highway 4, to reach Sydney at 3.25 pm. A morning bus leaves Sydney at 8.30 am, and travels the southern route to Port Hawkesbury. The afternoon bus leaves at 2 pm, and goes into North Sydney. Then it follows the TransCanada Highway, stops at Baddeck and Port Hawkesbury, and crosses the Canso Causeway.

Another way to reach Cape Breton is by private yacht or boat. Access to the Bras d'Or is through St Peter's Canal. There are a number of good harbours along the island's east and south coasts. Anyone intending to come by small boat is advised to secure a copy of *The Gulf of St Lawrence Pilot*, which covers Cape Breton and gives information on tides, currents, harbours, weather, anchorages, and other navigational matters. There are yacht clubs at Baddeck (Bras d'Or Club), Sydney (Dobson Yacht Club, Royal Cape Breton Yacht Club) and North Sydney (Northern Yacht Club).

GETTING AROUND THE ISLAND

It is almost impossible to 'do' Cape Breton without a car. There are car hire firms at Sydney Airport, Sydney, North Sydney and Port Hawkesbury. Limousine tours operate out of Sydney and Baddeck, and cabs are available on an hourly basis in Sydney. One trip from Sydney goes around the Cabot Trail four times a week; another takes in the Miners' Museum and Louisbourg, and goes three times a week.

There is good local bus service in Sydney, and throughout industrial Cape Breton. Buses connect Sydney with Glace Bay and Sydney Mines (via North Sydney), Sydney and West-mount, and Sydney and New Waterford. The rural bus services usually run only once or twice a day; they are operated mainly for people who want to come to Sydney to shop, or for services. A daily bus from Sydney goes to Baddeck, and then up to Margaree Forks. Another daily bus runs between Arichat and Sydney, leaving Arichat in the morning and returning there in the evening. Neither of these buses runs on Sunday. There is also a bus service between Sydney and Louisbourg that runs several times a day. A daily bus runs in the summer from Sydney to Dingwall, via Englishtown, Ingonish and Neil's Harbour; during the rest of the year it runs every second day. All buses out of Sydney start from the terminus, which is located on Bentinck Street in the centre of the city. A bus connects Port Hawkesbury and Inverness; it runs twice a day during the week and once on Sundays. This is the only bus service on the western side of the island.

Cape Breton should be seen from the sea, as the early settlers saw it. This can be done by hiring a boat or taking a boat trip. A boat trip to the Bird Islands off Cape Dauphin operates from Mountain View Lodge at Big Bras d'Or. Another boat trip takes visitors out from Baddeck, around Beinn Bhreagh, and back by way of the bird sanctuary on Spectacle Island. A two-hour pleasure cruise from the Canso Canal lock at Port Hastings takes in the new industrial complex along the strait.

Boats are available for hire, either for cruising or fishing, at Port Hood Island, Port Hawkesbury, Chéticamp, North Sydney, Sydney, Glace Bay, New Waterford, Mira Gut, Big Bras d'Or, Ingonish Beach, North Ingonish, Dingwall, Baddeck and Arichat.

The MV *St Ninian* is the only passenger vessel cruising the Bras d'Or. The ship, which is registered in Aberdeen, does a four-day cruise and a three-day cruise. The four-day cruise goes from North Sydney to Whycocomagh and Nyanza. At Baddeck, it anchors for two and a half hours, and entertainment from Gaelic College is brought on board. The ship then sails out through the Great Bras d'Or, calls at an outport in New-

175

foundland (St Albans on the Bay d'Espoir) and visits St Pierre. It returns to North Sydney to disembark passengers, and take on a new batch, then follows the same route, except for St Albans.

There are several good canoe routes on Cape Breton. One goes from Scotsville, at the head of Lake Ainslie, down the Margaree River to Margaree Forks, and can be done in three hours. Another short trip of five and a half hours is down the North-east Margaree from Portree to Margaree Forks. A two-day, twenty-six mile trip takes the canoeist down the Margaree River from Scotsville to Margaree Harbour. There is beautiful scenery and good trout and salmon fishing along the way. Anyone who wants to canoe, but not camp, can stay overnight at Margaree Lodge, Normaway Inn, Duck Cove Inn, or in other fine accommodation along the route.

One of the best canoe trips on the island is down the Mira, starting at Mira Lake. There are plenty of good campsites along the river, and no portaging is required. During the thirty-mile trip, the canoeist passes the site of early land grants (one to 'soldiers without fear, 1763'; another to 'married soldier without care'), the old French road, Captain Kidd's Rock near Marion Bridge (he is alleged to have visited the area), the site of buried treasure, the location of the oldest brick plant in North America where bricks were made for Louisbourg, and travels on down to the small settlement of Mira Gut. Details of these routes are contained in *Canoe Routes of Nova Scotia*, published by the Nova Scotia Canoeing Association in Halifax.

Cape Breton is marvellous hiking country. The sparsely settled parts of the island are accessible on foot, but the lakes and forests make it advisable to stick to existing trails which may be hard to find. There are more than twenty trails in the Cape Breton Highlands National Park, which are all well marked and signposted. Ten miles north of Baddeck is the Uisge Bhan Falls Walking Trail. From the provincial campsite at Whycoco-magh a trail leads to the top of Salt Mountain, and provides an excellent view over the Bras d'Or Lake. Cape North is accessible by a single road, and there is a walking trail to the top of Sugarloaf Mountain on Aspy Bay. The trail leads off the road from Cape North to Bay St Lawrence, about six miles from Cape North.

One of the most interesting trail systems runs down the west coast of the island, from Petit Etang, at the western entrance to the National Park, to Inverness, sixty miles to the south. This is the Acadian Trail. It links up with the Benn Bhiorach Trail, which connects Inverness and Mabou Harbour Mouth. The Acadian Trail is marked for the walker with signs and orange paint. It winds over beaches, grassland, paved highway, unpaved roads, up mountainsides and along beaches. A map of the trail can be obtained from the Canadian Youth Hostels Association, 6260 Quinpool Road, Halifax.

ACCOMMODATION

Cape Breton has a wide range of hotels, motels, guest houses, cabins, and trailer and camp sites. The Provincial government issues an excellent brochure called *Where To Stay in Nova Scotia* which is updated on the basis of information supplied by operators. Provincial hotel inspectors make regular checks. There is a tendency for the tourist beds to be located in certain centres. A motel opened in Louisbourg in 1972. Arichat had two motels in 1972, whereas Baddeck had thirteen establishments. There is accommodation at Bras d'Or, Big Bras d'Or, Briton Cove, Cape North, Chéticamp, Dingwall, Glace Bay, Indian Brook, Ingonish (ten establishments in all at Ingonish, Ingonish Beach, Ingonish Centre), Inverness, Iona, Louisbourg, Marble Mountain, Margaree (nine in all at the Forks, the Harbour and North-east Margaree), North Shore, North Sydney, Orangedale, Pleasant Bay, Port Hastings-Port Hawkesbury, Port Hood, Scotsville, St Ann's, South Gut, St Peter's, Sydney, West Bay and Whycocomagh.

The Province also issues a brochure on *Camp and Trailer Sites*. There were forty-four sites in operation on Cape Breton in 1972, with spaces for 2,068 tents and 1,363 trailers. Nova Scotia has stringent regulations for laying out tent and trailer parks, so that the traveller is assured of certain standards.

Between Port Hawkesbury and Glace Bay, there are sites at Dundee, Arichat, St Peter's, Ben Eoin, and Dominion; the park at St Peter's is run by the Provincial government. Between Port Hastings and Sydney, there are sites at Whycocomagh, South Lake Ainslie, Baddeck, Big Bras d'Or, Little Bras d'Or and North Sydney (both within two miles of the ferry dock). On the route between Port Hastings and Margaree Forks, up the west coast of the island, there are sites at Judique, Port Hood, and Dunvegan. There are five campsites in the Sydney-Louisbourg area—at Mira, Albert Bridge, Hillside Mira, and Catalone Gut.

The Cabot Trail is abundantly served by campgrounds and trailer sites. The privately owned sites on or near this route are at North-east Margaree, Margaree Forks, Margaree Harbour, Grand Etang, Chéticamp, Pleasant Bay, Ingonish Harbour (Smoky Ridge Park, with sites for 165 tents and 113 trailers, even has a swimming pool) and Indian Brook.

The National Park runs several campgrounds—at Chéticamp, Corney Brook, MacIntosh Brook, Big Intervale, Black Brook, Broad Cove and Ingonish Beach. People travelling in the park can only camp at these sites.

There are also picnic grounds run by the Province at Ben Eoin, Craigmore (thirteen miles west of Port Hastings), Mabou, South-west Margaree and Louisbourg. On or near the Cabot Trail there are picnic grounds at Harvard Lake, in the Rigwash Valley, at the Lone Shieling, at Sugar Loaf, South Mountain, Mary Ann Falls, Warren Lake, Clyburn Brook, Plaster and North River.

The Canadian Youth Hostels Association has hostels at Bras d'Or and Gardiner. The Canadian Restaurant Association issues a guide to eating out in Nova Scotia, but there are no gourmet restaurants on Cape Breton, and surprisingly very few specialising in seafood.

Most of the dozen or so museums are free, or cost only a nominal sum. They include the Salmon Museum at North-east Margaree, just off the Cabot Trail, which is sponsored by the Margaree Angler's Association. A museum of Cape Breton Heritage near by contains a display of tartans, textiles, weaving, hook rugs, and other material, as well as the drafts or patterns from which the immigrants wove coverlets. Down the road is the Old Time Country Store at Ross Section. At another museum everything that could be picked up locally has been piled into the building, including a book 'written by someone whose uncle lives here'. There is a wax museum just over the causeway at Port Hastings. Baddeck has the Alexander Graham Bell Museum. Another strikingly designed building is the Miners' Museum at Glace Bay. Visitors can go down the Ocean Deeps Colliery with guides who are ex-miners. The museum is free, but there is a charge for a visit to the colliery; boots, capes and hard hats are supplied. At Louisbourg, in addition to the fortress there is an information centre at the entrance to the town housed in the former railway station. At Arichat the Lenoire Forge contains material from the great days of sail. There is a Nicholas Denys Museum at St Peter's, and at Chéticamp a *Musée acadien*, a folk museum in the basement of the co-operative store that sells hooked rugs. At Margaree Harbour, the Elizabeth LeFort Gallery contains a selection of the work of this outstanding rug hooker from Chéticamp. At Mabou, the Pioneer's Shrine is full of intricate wood carving. At the Gaelic College at St Ann's there is the Giant MacAskill Highland Pioneers Museum. Among other things it contains MacAskill's clothes, chair, walking stick, bed—and original tombstone.

At Iona is the Highland Village. This sits on a hill with a

lovely view over Grand Narrows and the Bras d'Or Lakes. In the museum are relics of the early settlers, neatly laid out and labelled in English and Gaelic.

In Sydney, the Old Sydney Society runs St Patrick's Church Museum. This is housed in a charming little church, built in 1828, on the Esplanade beyond the Isle Royale Hotel. There are a few shattered gravestones in the small cemetery behind the church. One dated 1798 over a child's grave is inscribed with the cheerful admonition:

> Mourn Not for me, My Parents Dear
> I am not dead but sleeping here
> As I am now, so you must be
> Prepare for Death and follow me.

HUNTING AND FISHING

The Provincial Department of Lands and Forests is responsible for issuing hunting and fishing licences and for enforcement of regulations, except in the National Park, where this is a Federal responsibility. Up-to-date information on fishing and hunting seasons, bag limits for fish and game, and names of licensed guides can be obtained from the Department of Lands and Forests or the Nova Scotia Department of Tourism.

Neither game nor birds can be taken during the summer, nor may snares be set for any fur-bearing animal except between 1 November and 15 March. The deer season lasts from 15 October to 15 November. To hunt white-tailed deer, the visitor to the Province of Nova Scotia needs a non-resident big game licence. A small-game licence covers the hunting of snowshoe hares, Hungarian partridge, ruffed grouse, pheasant and a variety of waterfowl. The non-resident hunter must be accompanied by a guide.

Hunting is forbidden in the National Park, but fishing is allowed; a licence can be purchased from the office at either the Chéticamp or Ingonish park entrances. For fishing any-

180

where outside the park, the visitor to the Province should purchase a non-resident fishing licence. If a non-resident is going to cross areas where there is game to reach a fishing stream, he must be accompanied by a guide.

Boats can be rented by the hour or day for salt water fishing; most fish can be taken on tackle supplied by the boat master.

The highlight of any visit to Cape Breton is a trip around the Cabot Trail and it is best to allow a full day for the 184 miles of mountainous highway. This road goes north through the Margaree Valley, and along the coast to Chéticamp, a long street of a settlement. Here the Acadian flag flies in front of some of the houses. St Peter's Church is an impressive stone building completed in 1892, at a cost of $40,000 (£16,000). Now, the local people say, it costs as much to paint as it did to build it. Chéticamp has a thriving hooked rug industry, and this is the best place to buy these beautiful handcrafts. Just north of Chéticamp, the trail enters the Cape Breton Highlands National Park, climbs over a couple of mountains (French Mountain, whose 1,492ft summit is the highest highway point in Nova Scotia, and Mount MacKenzie with a summit at 1,222ft) and then descends into Pleasant Bay, which is outside the park boundaries. Four miles west of Pleasant Bay there is a roadside picnic shelter, a replica in stone of the huts used by Scottish crofters when tending their sheep. Its name, The Lone Shieling, comes from 'Canadian Boat Song':

> From the lone shieling of the misty island
> Mountains divide us, and the waste of seas;
> Yet still the blood is strong, the heart is Highland,
> And in our dreams we behold the Hebrides.

The trail swings eastward up the slopes of North Mountain to an elevation of 1,460ft, then descends the North Aspy Valley.

This opens out to the Atlantic, and is known also as Sunrise Valley for the beauty of the sunrises here. At the head of the valley a group of young craftsmen make and sell stained-glass lamps and wall ornaments, and wooden toys without nails. Their workshop is called 'Suxtaglume', which despite its medieval sound is coined from contemporary slang, 'sucks to gloom'. From here the trail loops through Cape North, and crosses a lunar landscape where the gypsum has been mined. From here, two interesting side trips can be taken to Dingwall, a small fishing village, and to Bay St Lawrence at the northern tip of the island.

From Cape North, the trail follows the northern boundary of the National Park; Neil's Harbour, another small fishing village, lies just off the trail, near the Buchanan Memorial Hospital. The Cabot Trail then follows the coast through the National Park, via the main streets of the various Ingonishes— Ingonish, Ingonish Centre, Ingonish Beach, South Ingonish Harbour, and Ingonish Ferry. The park headquarters is just south of Ingonish Beach, and here the trail leaves the park. It winds around Ingonish Harbour, past the Mount Smoky Ski Lodge, and climbs over Smoky, the prominent headland that dominates the coast in this region. Here the road drops 1,200ft in 1·3 miles. It then runs along the narrow strip of land between the plateau edge and the sea, strikes inland up the valley of the Barachois River and goes over to the head of the northern arm of St Ann's Harbour. It follows the shores of the harbour, passes Gaelic College and Norman McLeod's country, and joins the TransCanada Highway at South Gut St Ann's. From here the traveller can return to Baddeck, or turn left and go on to Sydney.

CAPE BRETON HIGHLANDS NATIONAL PARK

The Canadian government's policy for the national parks has three main goals—resource conservation, interpretation and development. The main idea is to keep certain parts of Canada in their original condition; wildflowers may not be picked in the Cape Breton Highlands National Park, nor may rocks be removed. The park was established on 23 June 1936. The first land was acquired in May 1935, and the park now covers about 370 square miles. It encompasses a wide range of habitats—the steeply tilted beds of sedimentary rocks at Presqu'ile, the treeless barrens of the interior, the deep valleys of such rivers as the Mackenzie, the small beaches along the Atlantic and the Gulf of St Lawrence, and the virgin hardwoods at the base of North Mountain. The theme of the park is 'Where the Mountains Meet the Sea'. It is laid out to be seen and appreciated, and there is an interpretation and information centre at the park headquarters at Ingonish Beach. Outdoor theatres for films and slide shows are being developed at the major campgrounds. There are outdoor theatres at Ingonish Beach, Broad Cove, and Chéticamp.

But the best way to see the environment is on foot. About twenty trails, of varying degrees of difficulty, lead into the park. From the east end of the Chéticamp campgrounds in the park the Salmon Pools Trail goes up the Chéticamp River. This is an easy walk between the high steep banks of the river. The Lake Trail starts from the same place, but climbs 1,500ft in three and a half miles and continues for another mile and a half on the plateau top. This is a difficult climb and takes four to five hours. The Fishing Cove Trail, which starts off the Cabot Trail about four miles south of Pleasant Bay, drops 1,100ft in two and a half miles.

On the eastern side of the park, it is possible to drive (slowly and carefully) part of the way along the Lake of Islands Road, and then to take the trail that leads into the dry barrens at 1,200ft to 1,400ft. About three miles north of the park head-quarters, a trail leads up to Mount Franey Fire Tower at 1,405ft. There are numerous short trails leading into the park and through a variety of habitats from inland barrens to beaches on this side of the park.

There are interpretive walks, conducted by park personnel with talks in English and French. Among these is the Coastal Wonderland Walk on the eastern side of the park, which goes through a winter 'moose yard', young mixed woods, and one of the two Jack Pine forests known on Cape Breton Island, and along beautiful coastal headlands. The 'Living Waters' walk starts and ends at the Exhibit Centre at Ingonish Beach, crossing salt water beach, barachois, and marshes. On the western side there is the Acadian Grove, and an interpretive tour of Presqu'ile, which has a varied habitat. A motor tour, starting at the information bureau, travels for seven miles along the Cabot Trail, examining the geological history of the area.

Information on the timing and scheduling of the tours and walks is posted on bulletin boards or can be obtained from the park staff.

There are also self-guiding tours. A printed guide is available at the start of the Green Cove Trail, about four miles south of Neil's Harbour. This trail explores a coastal headland. The trees here are dwarfed and twisted from wind and salt, and are known as *krummholz* (German for 'crooked wood'). There is a cobble beach, and a wide variety of headland plants—bayberry, crowberry, hairgrass, juniper and cinquefoil. Where there is no soil, the foundations of the island are exposed—pink granite with large feldspar crystals, granitic gneiss, and intrusions of pegmatite, or coarse red granite. A small sand beach is the site of only two grasses—American dunegrass and American beachgrass. There is even a fenced-off patch of poison ivy along the trail.

THE FORTRESS OF LOUISBOURG

In 1961, a minute of the Canadian Cabinet stated, 'The Fortress of Louisbourg is to be restored partially so that future generations can thereby see and understand the role of the fortress as a hinge of history. The restoration is to be carried out so that the lessons of history can be animated.' And so began a project that to the end of 1971 had cost about $20 million (£8 million). With painstaking almost obsessional care, archaeologists, historians, engineers, draughtsmen, ex-miners and others are slowly rebuilding the Louisbourg of 1745, when the fortress and town were in their prime. The project was initiated, in part, to provide work and retraining for unemployed coal miners, who learned how to cut stone, to fashion wood beams with axes, and to roof buildings in the eighteenth-century style. Rebuilding Louisbourg involved excavations on the spot—thousands of artifacts were recovered, and the place of every stone had to be noted. It also involved careful examination of over 350,000 documents, maps, charts, plans and other records. Louisbourg became something of an historian's and archaeologist's nightmare, and is emerging as a tourist's dream.

Louisbourg is twenty-four miles south of Sydney, and the fortress lies opposite the modern town, at the southern entrance to the wide harbour. Cars must be parked at the reception centre, and a bus takes visitors into the fortress. Work has focussed on the citadel, the most prominent feature of the fortress, which contains the Château St Louis and the King's Bastion, and represented the core of the defensive system, and the Dauphin Demi-Bastion at the landward entrance. The massive walls look impregnable from the landward side. But even the unskilled eye soon picks out the weakness of the fortress —its exposure to the sea, the isolation of the Royal Battery and the Island Battery, the way in which the walls could be commanded from the low hills behind the fortress. Reconstruction is also going on in that part of the town that lies between the King's Bastion and the harbour. In all about a quarter of the fortress and town will be restored, hopefully by the end of the 1970s.

Complete authenticity is the keynote at Fortress Louisbourg: the beams are hand-hewn and held together with wooden pegs.

The nails are hand-made replicas of the originals. Herbs scent the air in the kitchen, but the restorers have mercifully not recreated the smell of drying cod that hung over Louisbourg like a miasma, and added to the woes of the residents of this remote rocky spot. Even before restoration has been completed, swallows have installed themselves under the eaves, and swoop around, bringing the first permanent life to the old town.

In the Château St Louis, things are as they were when the French were in residence. A number of rooms have been furnished—kitchens, officers' quarters, prisons, dining rooms, council chambers. The luxury of the governor's quarters contrasts with the bareness of the men's barracks. When Governor Du Quesnel died in his bedroom on 9 October 1744, he left behind fifty embroidered shirts, ninety-nine handkerchiefs and ten pairs of slippers. The chapel has been restored, and has the scrubbed look of fresh pine. Louis XV peers down from behind the altar. His portrait is everywhere—bewigged, richly clothed, gazing out of the frame in an abstracted manner, perhaps wondering why so much of his money was spent so unwisely.

One visitors' shelter near the former museum (now housing food concessions) contains Katherine MacLennan's model of the town and the fortress. Senator John S. MacLennan wrote the definitive book on Louisbourg, and both he and his daughter played a large role in helping to preserve the fortress for the nation.

Areas being excavated or reconstructed are fenced off, but this still gives plenty of scope for rambling over the site. Visitors can wander out to Rochefort Point, down streets where no houses now stand, past the site of the hospital, and see where many of the French, New Englanders and English lie buried. And around the King's Bastion, staff in costume help to re-create Louisbourg as it was, filled with people. The programme of 'animation' began in 1971, and puts new life into the old grey walls.

Newspapers, radio and television pour out a steady stream of information about what is happening on the island. *The Cape Breton Post* is published daily except Sunday in Sydney. *The Cape Breton Highlander* comes out once a week and contains a blend of fact and opinion that reflects the thoughts of many Cape Bretoners. The *Richmond Record* is published once a week at Arichat, and *The Scotia Sun* is another weekly that appears in Port Hawkesbury.

There are three AM stations and one FM station. One AM station (CBI) is run by the Canadian Broadcasting Corporation. Another, CHER, concentrates on local matters, with broadcasts in English, French, Gaelic and Micmac. There is a private TV station (CJCB) at Sydney, and a CBC TV station. Chéticamp receives a French-language TV channel.

The National Parks put out a great deal of tourist material. A brochure on Louisbourg, a booklet on the Alexander Graham Bell Museum, and maps of the walking trails in the Cape Breton Highlands National Park are available free of charge. The Provincial government is also generous with its tourist publications. The Department of Tourism (PO Box 130, Halifax, Nova Scotia) issues a highways map, *Outdoors in Nova Scotia*; an excellent 128-page *Tour Book*; a *Calendar of Events*, and a guide to *Salt Water Fishing*, in addition to *Where to Stay* and *Camp and Trailer Sites*. DEVCO publishes an excellent free map of Cape Breton Island, with the points of interest marked. This material can be picked up at the information booths at the entry points to Cape Breton at Port Hawkesbury and North Sydney.

BIBLIOGRAPHY

The island of Cape Breton has inspired a variety of people to put pen to paper. The most comprehensive history of the island up to 1870 was written by Richard Brown, manager of the General Mining Association, while Senator John S. McLennan wrote the definitive book on Fortress Louisbourg (1918). There have been a number of valuable local histories. Father Chiasson's history of Chéticamp is an outstanding work, unfortunately not available in English. John Hart was an active participant and observer of many of the events recorded in his *History of Northeast Margaree*. Visitors too wrote of the island. Ensign Prenties, who arrived on Cape Breton via a shipwreck, gives an understandably jaundiced description; the account (1874) by Charles Dudley Warner, one of the first tourists, has a faintly patronising air to it; while that by Gordon Brinley (1936) is full of enthusiasm.

There have been a number of overall studies of the Maritimes, of Eastern Nova Scotia, and of parts of Cape Breton Island. The Atlantic Development Board has produced a series of thick reports on fisheries, agriculture, mineral resources, etc, in the four Atlantic Provinces. In 1966, the Institute of Public Affairs at Dalhousie University received a contract to undertake a number of studies in the nine North-eastern Counties of Nova Scotia that formed a 'Pilot Research Region'. Reports were issued on the human and natural resources of the region that put a lot of useful data between two covers. The Federal government has also financed research by the St Francis Xavier University Extension Division on the island, and studies of resources in Inverness County and southern Cape Breton have been published.

Canada carries out a full census every ten years and a less detailed one every five years. The results of the 1971 full census were still appearing when this book went to press. Statistics Canada in Halifax supplied us with all the data that were available. Additional statistics were obtained from the Provincial Department of Development in Sydney and Halifax.

BIBLIOGRAPHY

In Halifax, the best collections of material on Cape Breton Island can be found in the Legislative Library and the Public Archives of Nova Scotia. In Sydney, good sources are the James McConnell Memorial Library and Xavier College Library and Cape Bretoniana Collection. The Special Collection in the Library at St Francis Xavier University is also very useful.

The following bibliography is 'selected' rather than 'exhaustive', since it contains only items consulted during the preparation of this book.

ARNOLD, MARY E. *The Story of Tompkinsville.* New York, 1940
ATLANTIC DEVELOPMENT BOARD. *Annual Report 1968–69.* Ottawa, 1969
———. *Fisheries in the Atlantic Provinces.* Ottawa, 1969
———. *Forestry in the Atlantic Provinces.* Ottawa, 1968
———. *Mineral Resources of the Atlantic Provinces.* Ottawa, 1969
———. *Profiles of Education in the Atlantic Provinces.* Ottawa, 1969
ATLANTIC PROVINCES ECONOMIC COUNCIL. *Annual Report 1970–71.*
Atlantic Yearbook 1971. Fredericton, 1971
BAGNELL, KENNETH. 'The Evening Town I Knew As Morning', *The Globe Magazine* 10 October 1972
BAIRD, DAVID M. *Cape Breton Highlands National Park: Where the Mountains Meet the Sea.* Ottawa, 1965
———. *A Guide to Geology for Visitors in Canada's National Parks.* Ottawa, 1963
BAKER, W. J. *The History of the Marconi Company.* 1970
BECK, J. MURRAY. *The Government of Nova Scotia.* Toronto, 1957
BIRD, WILL R. 'Nova Scotia's Highland Cape Breton', *Canadian Geographical Journal*, 38 (1949), 78–91
BLAKELEY, PHYLLIS R. *Nova Scotia's Two Remarkable Giants.* Windsor, N.S., 1970
BOLLES, FRANK. *From Blomidon to Cape Smoky.* Boston, 1895
BOUGHNER, C. C. 'The Climate of the Atlantic Provinces', *Public Affairs*, 3 (1940), 114–18
BOURINOT, John C. *Historical and Descriptive Account of the Island of Cape Breton and of its Memorials of the French Regime.* Montreal, 1892
———. 'The Island of Cape Breton: The "Long Wharf" of the Dominion', *Canadian Monthly and National Review* (1882), 329–38
———. 'Notes on a Ramble Through Cape Breton', *The New Dominion Monthly*, 2 (1869), 87–92
BOYLE, GEORGE. *Father Tompkins of Nova Scotia.* New York, 1953

BIBLIOGRAPHY

BREBNER, JOHN B. *The Explorers of North America, 1742–1806.* 1955
——. *New England's Outpost: Acadia Before the Conquest of Canada.* New York, 1927
BRINLEY, GORDON. *Away to Cape Breton.* Toronto, 1936
BROWN, RICHARD. *The Coal Fields and Coal Trade of the Island of Cape Breton.* 1871
——. *A History of the Island of Cape Breton.* 1869
CAMERON, AUSTIN W. *A Guide to Eastern Canadian Mammals.* Ottawa, 1956
CAMPBELL, G. G. (ed). *Ensign Prenties's Narrative: A Castaway on Cape Breton.* Toronto, 1968
CAMPBELL, M. R. 'A History of Basic Steel Manufacturing at Sydney, Nova Scotia', *Mining Society of Nova Scotia Transactions,* 55 (1952), 217–25
CANADA. DEPT OF INDIAN AFFAIRS AND NORTHERN DEVELOPMENT. *Indians of Quebec and the Maritime Provinces: An Historical Review.* Ottawa, 1971
CANADA. DEPT OF TRANSPORT. *Report of the Task Force-Operation Oil Clean-up of the 'Arrow' Oil Spill in Chedabucto Bay,* 3 vols. Ottawa, 1970
CANADIAN HYDROGRAPHIC SERVICE. *Gulf of St Lawrence Pilot,* 6th ed. Ottawa, 1968
CANADIAN NATIONAL RAILWAYS, RESEARCH AND DEVELOPMENT DEPT. *Industrial Survey of the Strait of Canso Area and the Town of Port Hawkesbury and Mulgrave.* Montreal, 1967
CANADIAN WELFARE COUNCIL. *A Preliminary Report of Poverty in Four Selected Areas.* Ottawa, 1965
CANN, D. B., MacDOUGALL, J. I., and HILCHEY, J. D. *Soil Survey of Cape Breton Island.* Truro N.S., 1963
CAPE BRETON DEVELOPMENT CORPORATION. *Annual Reports.* Sydney, 1967
'Cape Breton Export Pulpwood Market', *Woodland Ledger,* 72 (1972), 7
Cape Breton Highlands National Park Public Hearing, 24 June 1970. *Transcript of Proceedings.* Sydney, 1970
Cape Breton Regional Health Services. 3 vols. Halifax, 1972
'Cape Breton's Deserted Mining Town, Broughton', *Montreal Daily Star,* (25 May 1907)
CHIASSON, ANSELME. *Chéticamp: Histoire et Traditions acadiennes,* 3rd ed. Moncton, 1972

CLARK, ANDREW H. *Acadia: The Geography of Early Nova Scotia to 1760.* Madison, 1968

COADY, MOSES M. *Masters of Their Own Destiny: The Story of the Antigonish Movement.* New York, 1939

COCHRAN, CLAY L. *Co-operative Self-Help in Nova Scotia.* Washington DC, 1968

CREIGHTON, HELEN. *Bluenose Ghosts.* Toronto, 1957

CREIGHTON, HELEN, and MACLEOD, CALUM. *Gaelic Songs in Nova Scotia.* Ottawa, 1964

CUJES, RUDI. *Fisherman's Co-operatives in Nova Scotia.* Montreal, nd

CUMMING, PETER A. et al (eds). *Native Rights in Canada,* 2nd ed. Toronto, 1972

DENNIS, CLARA. *Cape Breton Over.* Boston, 1942

DIMOCK, CELIA C. *Isle Royale: 'The Front Door of Canada'.* Halifax, nd

DONALD, J. R. *The Cape Breton Coal Problem.* Ottawa, 1966

DOUCET, L. J. *The Road to the Isle: 'The World's Deepest Causeway'.* Fredericton, 1955

DOWNEY, FAIRFAX. *Louisbourg: Key to a Continent.* Englewood Cliffs, NJ, 1965

DUNN, CHARLES W. *The Highland Settler: Portrait of the Scottish Gael in Nova Scotia.* Toronto, 1953

ERSKINE, J. S. 'Early Cultures of Nova Scotia: Cape Breton', *Journal of Education,* 5th ser. 19 (1970), 34–6

EVANS, G. N. D. *Uncommon Obdurate: The Several Public Careers of J. F. W. DesBarres.* Salem, Mass. and Toronto, 1969

EVANS, REGINALD. 'Transportation and Communication in Nova Scotia', Master's Thesis. Dalhousie Univ, Halifax, 1936

FERGUSON, C. BRUCE. *The Boundaries of Nova Scotia and its Counties.* Halifax, 1966

——. *The Inauguration of the Free School System in Nova Scotia.* Halifax, 1964

——. *Local Government in Nova Scotia.* Halifax, 1961

FLETCHER, HUGH. *Report on the Geology of Northern Cape Breton.* Montreal, 1884

FORSEY, EUGENE. *Economic and Social Aspects of the Nova Scotia Coal Industry.* Montreal, 1925

FRASER, MARY L. *Folk Lore of Nova Scotia.* np, nd

GOLDTHWAIT, J. W. *Physiography of Nova Scotia.* Ottawa, 1924

GOW, JOHN. *Cape Breton Illustrated: Historic Picturesque and Descriptive.* Toronto, 1893

Graham, Gerald S. *Empire of the North Atlantic: The Maritime Struggle for North America.* Toronto, 1950

GRAY, FRANCIS. *The Coal-fields and Coal Industry of Eastern Canada.* Ottawa, 1917

GRAY, F. W. 'The Future of the Sydney Coalfield', *Dalhousie Review,* 21 (1941), 178–83

GREEN, H. GORDON. *A Heritage of Canadian Handicrafts.* Toronto, 1967

HAIGH, K. R. *Cable Ships and Submarine Cables.* 1968

HARRINGTON, LYN. 'The Cabot Trail', *Canadian Geographical Jnl,* 36 (1948), 204–21

HART, JOHN F. *History of Northeast Margaree.* np, 1963

HARVEY, A. S. *Human Resources of North Eastern Nova Scotia.* Halifax, 1969

HARVEY, DANIEL C. 'Educational Activities in Cape Breton, 1758–1850', *Journal of Education,* 4th ser. 6 (1935), 518–32

——. 'Scottish Immigration to Cape Breton', *Dalhousie Review,* 21 (1941), 313–24

——. 'The Wreck of the *Astraea*', *Dalhousie Review,* 21 (1941), 217–14

—— (comp). *Holland's Description of Cape Breton Island and Other Documents.* Halifax, 1935

—— (ed). *Letters of the Rev Norman McLeod, 1835–51.* Halifax, 1939

HARVEY, E. ROY. *Sydney, Nova Scotia: An Urban Study.* Toronto, 1971

HAWBOLDT, L. S., and BULMER, R. M. *The Forest Resources of Nova Scotia.* Halifax, 1958

'Here come the Supertankers', *Commentator,* 30 (1971), 4–7

HOGAN, ANDREW. *Teach-in: The Sydney Steel Crisis.* Halifax, 1967

HUDSON, S. C., and LEWIS, J. N. 'The Quest for Income in Rural Cape Breton', *Public Affairs,* 4 (1940), 12–14

INNIS, Harold A. *The Cod Fisheries: The History of an International Economy.* Toronto, 1940

Jackson, Elva E. *Cape Breton and the Jackson Kith and Kin.* Windsor NS, 1971

JOHNSON, DOUGLAS. *The New England-Acadia Shoreline.* New York, 1925, facsimile 1967

JOHNSTON, ANGUS A. *A History of the Catholic Church in Eastern Nova Scotia.* Antigonish, vol 1, 1960; vol 2, 1971

KONTAK, W. J. F., and LEBLANC, J. ARTHUR. *A Survey of the Fishing Industry of Eastern Nova Scotia.* Sydney, 1960

LAIDLAW, ALEX (ed). *The Man from Margaree: Writings and Speeches of M. M. Coady.* Toronto, 1971

LEBLANC, EMERY. *Les Acadiens.* Montreal, 1963

LUNN, JOHN. 'Louisbourg: The Emerging Touchstone', *Canadian Antiques Collector*, 7 (1972), 37–40

McCAWLEY, STUART. *Cape Breton, Come All Ye.* Glace Bay, 1966

MACDONALD, A. A., and CLARE, W. B. *North Inverness Resource Survey.* Antigonish, 1966

——. *South Inverness Resource Survey.* Antigonish, 1966

MACDONALD, H. H. *The Royal Isle.* Antigonish, 1970

MACDOUGALL, JOHN L. *History of Inverness County, Nova Scotia.* Truro NS, 1922

MACKENZIE, CATHERINE D. 'The Charm of Cape Breton Island', *National Geographic Mag*, 38 (1920), 34–60

MACKLEY, M. FLORENCE. 'Folk Art in Cape Breton', *Canadian Antiques Collector*, 7 (1972), 57–9

MACKINNON, JONATHAN G. *Old Sydney.* Sydney, 1918

MACLENNAN, HUGH. 'Cape Breton: The Legendary Island', *Saturday Night*, 66 (1951), 12–13

——. 'The Cabot', *Macleans Magazine*, 78 (1965), 13–14

——. *Each Man's Son.* Toronto, 1951

McLENNAN, JOHN S. *Louisbourg from its Foundation to its Fall, 1713–1758.* 1918; reprinted Sydney, 1969

MACNEIL, NEIL. *The Highland Heart in Nova Scotia.* 1948, Canadian edition Toronto, 1971

MACPHAIL, MARGARET. *Loch Bras d'Or.* Windsor NS, 1970

McPHERSON, FLORA. *Watchman Against the World: The Story of Norman McLeod and His People.* Toronto, 1962

McTAGGART-COWAN, P. D. 'Pollution or Poppycock', *Canadian Geographical Jnl*, 84 (1972), 174–87

MARTIN, J. LYNTON. *The Amphibians and Reptiles of Nova Scotia.* Halifax, nd

MARX, ROBERT F. *Shipwrecks of the Western Hemisphere.* New York, 1971

MATHIAS, PHILIP. *Forced Growth; Five Studies of Government Involvement in the Development of Canada.* Toronto, 1971

MORGAN, ROBERT. 'Joseph Frederick Wallet DesBarres and the Founding of the Cape Breton Colony', *Revue de L'Univ d'Ottawa*, 39 (1969), 212-27

MORRISON, SAMUEL E. *The European Discovery of America: The Northern Voyages, AD 500–1600.* New York, 1971

M

BIBLIOGRAPHY

MURRAY, JOHN. *The History of the Presbyterian Church in Cape Breton.* Truro, NS, 1921

NICHOLS, George E. 'The Vegetation of Northern Cape Breton Island, Nova Scotia', *Trans of the Connecticut Academy of Arts and Science*, 22 (1918), 249–67

NOVA SCOTIA. DEPT OF DEVELOPMENT. *County Surveys.* Halifax, 1970

NOVA SCOTIA. DEPT OF EDUCATION. *Amalgamation of School Boards.* Halifax, 1970

—— *Province of Nova Scotia Directory of Schools in Operation 1971–72.* Halifax, 1971

NOVA SCOTIA. DEPT OF LANDS AND FOREST. *Notes on Nova Scotia Wildlife.* Kentville, 1968

NOVA SCOTIA. DEPT OF MINES. *Geology of Nova Scotia.* Halifax, nd

NOVA SCOTIA. DEPT OF MUNICIPAL AFFAIRS. *Annual Report of Municipal Statistics for the Year 1970.* Halifax, 1971

NOVA SCOTIA. PUBLIC ARCHIVES. *Place-names and Places of Nova Scotia.* Halifax, 1967

NOVA SCOTIA. ROYAL COMMISSION ON PUBLIC SCHOOL FINANCE IN NOVA SCOTIA. *Report.* Halifax, 1954

Parker, John P. *Cape Breton, Ships and Men.* Toronto, 1967

PARKIN, JOHN H. *Bell and Baldwin: Their Development of Aerodromes and Hydrodomes at Baddeck, Nova Scotia.* Toronto, 1964

PATTERSON, C. A. 'Dosco', *Atlantic Advocate*, 50 (1960), 38–40

Portugaliae Monumenta Cartographica, 5 vols. Lisbon, 1960

PUTNAM, D. F. 'The Climate of the Maritimes Provinces', *Canadian Geographical Jnl*, 21 (1940), 134–47

QUINPOOL, JOHN. *First Things in Acadia.* Halifax, 1936

'Reflections on Canso Strait', *Commentator*, 30 (1971), 2–3

RUSSELL, FRANKLIN. *The Atlantic Coast.* The Illustrated National History of Canada. Toronto, 1970

ST FRANCIS XAVIER UNIV. EXTENSION DIV. *Local Government in the Changing Economy of Industrial Cape Breton.* Finnis Report, Sydney, 1968

'Search for New Uses of Strontium Compounds', *Science Forum*, 4 (1971), 32

SHIELDS, W. D., and VEINOT, J. A. *Strait of Canso Fish Farm Feasibility Study.* Dartmouth NS, 1969

STEVENS, G. R. *Canadian National Railways:* vol 2. *Towards the Inevitable.* Toronto, 1962

STORM, ALEX. *Canada's Treasure Hunt.* Winnipeg, 1967

194

Strait of Canso Steering Committee. *Local Government Review*. Halifax, 1971

THOMAS, C. A. 'Highway Development in Nova Scotia', *Proceedings Nova Scotia Community Planning Conference*. (1964)

'The Treasure of *Chameau*', *Nova Scotia Magazine*, 3 (1972), 16–17

TUFTS, ROBIE W. *The Birds of Nova Scotia*. Halifax, 1961

UNIACKE, RICHARD J. *Uniacke's Sketches of Cape Breton and Other Papers Relating to Cape Breton Island*. Halifax, 1958

VERNON, CHARLES W. *Cape Breton, Canada at the Beginning of the Twentieth Century*. Toronto, 1903

WALLIS, W. D., and WALLIS, R. S. *The Micmac Indians of Eastern Canada*. Minneapolis, 1955

WALWORTH, ARTHUR. *Cape Breton, Isle of Romance*. Toronto, 1948

WARNER, CHARLES D. *Baddeck and That Sort of Thing*. Boston, 1874

WILLIAMSON, JAMES A. *The Cabot Voyages and the Bristol Discovery Under Henry VII*. Cambridge, 1962

WOMEN'S INSTITUTE OF NOVA SCOTIA, LOUISBOURG BRANCH. *Louisbourg, 1758–1958*. Louisbourg, 1958

——, MIRA GUT BRANCH. 'History of Mira Gut, 1758–1968' Mimeo

WOOD, K. S., and PALMER, J. *Natural Resources of Northeastern Nova Scotia*. Halifax, 1970

WUORIO, EVA-LIS. 'Cape Breton: Into the Land of Mod', *Maclean's Mag*, 63 (1950), 16–17

ACKNOWLEDGEMENTS

We received a great deal of help and co-operation while preparing this book. People, except in isolated cases, were never too busy to stop and talk, to identify a source, or to help in locating photos.

Miss Mary Fraser, Chief Librarian, Cape Breton Regional Library was an enthusiastic and knowledgeable source of information on the island and was never stumped by our questtions. She and her staff went to endless trouble on our behalf. Dr Bruce Ferguson and his staff at the Public Archives provided excellent service, as did the staff of the St Francis Xavier University Library at Antigonish. Mrs Grace MacKinnon of the Regional Library at Antigonish very kindly got material for us on interlibrary loan, and Miss Shirley Elliott, the Legislative Librarian of Nova Scotia, was also most helpful.

Many Federal and Provincial government officials went to a great deal of trouble to tell us about the island, and to supply us with data: Mr J. F. Amirault, Halifax Airport; Mr William Butler, Department of Development, Sydney; Mr N. G. C. Campbell and Mrs Evelyn Cole, Statistics Canada, Halifax; Mr Eric Dennis, Nova Scotia Communications and Information Centre; Mr L. Ells, Department of Agriculture, Sydney; Mr Peter G. Hebb, Nova Scotia Power Commission; Mr D. G. Keenan, Department of Education, Halifax; Mr Evan Lloyd, Department of Tourism, Sydney; Mr Bob McGregor, Lands and Forest, Sydney; Mr D. T. McNeil, Fisheries Protection, Sydney; Mr John A. MacPherson, Atomic Energy of Canada, Glace Bay; Mr George Rochester, former Superintendent,

ACKNOWLEDGEMENTS

Cape Breton Highlands National Park; Mr Ray Stone, Department of Transport, Ottawa; Mr Neil Van Nostrand, Lands and Forests, Kentville; Mr P. A. Wright, Department of Highways, Sydney.

At the Fortress of Louisbourg, Dr John Lunn, Mr D. M. Lohnes and Dr Bob Morgan gave us every assistance. At DEVCO, Mr John Teeter, Mr David Dow and Mr Karl Turner were most helpful, as was Dr John Jenness, formerly of DEVCO.

In the private sector, Mr David Newton, formerly of *The Cape Breton Post*, Mr C. Ray Peters of the Industrial Cape Breton Board of Trade, and Mr Roy Gould of the Union of Nova Scotia Indians were extremely co-operative. We are also very grateful for the help given by: Mrs Ellen Arsenault, Coady International Institute; Mr D. G. Berry, Gulf Oil Canada at Point Tupper; Père Anselme Chiasson, Capucin, Moncton; Mr George Chiasson, Sydney; Mr Doug Lacombe, CNR, Moncton; Mr Paul MacEwan, MLA, Sydney; Mr Jim Mac-Millan, Old Sydney Society; Mr Angus John MacNeil; Mr S. R. MacNeil, Curator, Highland Village, Iona; Mr J. F. Marshall, Maritime Telegraph and Telephone Co, Halifax; Messrs Maguire and Wilbur of *Railroad Magazine*, New York; Mr Charlie Musial of the Cape Breton Wildlife Association; Miss Margaret Sexton, Sydney; Mr Simon White, Cape Breton Regional Planning Commission; Mr R. D. Tennant, the *Maritime Express*, Halifax.

We would also like to thank the many other people, on and off the island, who gave us their views and those little bits of information that helped us to make sense of our impressions, and Mrs Pat Van de Sande, who typed the manuscript swiftly and efficiently.

None of the individuals mentioned is responsible for any errors, omissions, or misunderstandings that may be contained in this book.

INDEX

The numbers in italics refer to illustrations

DEVCO, 29, 84, 85, 93, 95, 111–13, 117, 126, 137
Diabetes, 143
Dijon, 171
Dingwall, 17, 122, 135, 175, 182
DISCO, 59–60
Dominion, 104, 120, 127
Dominion Coal Company, 59, 85, 103
Dominion Iron and Steel Company, 59–60
Dominion Steel and Coal Corporation, *see* DOSCO
Donald, J. R., 111
'Donald from Bras d'Or', 65
Donkin, 120, 138
DOSCO, 60, 109, 110, 111
Draggers, 92
Drucour, Augustin de, 47
Drucour, Madame de, 48
Du Chambon, Dupont, 46
Ducks, 36
Duncan Commission, 61, 99–100
Dunvegan, 13
Du Quesnel, Jean Baptiste, 44ff, 186
Dutch, 23, 144
Dykes (geological), 15

East Bay, 64, 78, 120, 162
East Bay Hills, 17
Eastern Counties Regional Library, 138
Eastern Provincial Airways, 172
Eastern Telephone Company, 79
Eastern Trust Company, 89
Edinburgh Castle, 41
Education, 132–8
Edward VII, 80
Eels, 37, 91
Eigg, 156
85th Nova Scotia Highlanders, 107
Electric street railway, 86
Elizabeth LeFort Gallery, 179
Elk Island National Park, Alberta, 35
Employment, 103–4, 107–9
English Harbour, 41, 43
Englishtown, 13, 79, 168, 175; ferry, 20, 83
Enon Lake, 112
Enterprise (ship), 67
Erskine, J. S., 39
Eskasoni Indian Reserve, 93, 148
Evangelical United Brethren, 163

Fagundes, Joao Alvares, 41
Fairlie Patent locomotives, 85
Family Services of Eastern Nova Scotia, 129
Farms and farming, *see* Agriculture

Farquharson, Alexander, 162
Fedora, Nicolas, 157
Fernandez, Joao, 13
Ferries, 66–8, 83, 173
Feversham (ship), 171
Fidelity (ship), 68
Fiset, Father Pierre, 151, 165
Fish, 37–8, 40–1
Fisheries Protection Service, 128
Fishing, 40–1, 90–3, 100; *see also* Angling
Fishing Cove Trail, 183
'Flakes' (drying stages), 41
Florence, 121, 138
Forest fires, 31
Forest inventory, 96–7
Forests and forestry, 30–1, 95–9, 184
Fortress of Louisbourg National Historic Park, 84, *69, 70,* 116, 170, 174, 184–6, 187
Fourchu, 84
Framboise, 13
Fraser, Bishop William, 161
Fredericton, 172
Free Schools Act (1864), 133
French, 41–8, 90, 146
French (language), 133, 151, 187
French Mountain, 181
Frenchvale, 156
Frogs, 35
Fur trade, 90

Gabarus, 84; Bay, 21
Gaelic, 13, 55, 75, 144, 153–5, 156, 157, 162, 166, 187
Gaelic College, St Ann's, 154, 175, 179, 182
Gaelic Society of Cape Breton, 154, 155
Gales, 29, 30
Game, 180
Gander, 172
General Instruments of Canada, 112
General Mining Association (GMA), 59, 79, 84, 85
George II, 48
Germany, 157
Gilbert, Sir Humphrey, 158
Glace Bay, 79ff, 86, 92, 93, 95, 107, 108, 118–19, 120, 121, 129, 144, 174, 175
Glace Bay Hospital, 144
Glacial till, 23
Glaciation, 18–19
Glasgow Normal School, 133
Glasgow University, Department of Celtic Studies, 153
Glencoe Mills, 97, 108
Glendale, 156

INDEX

INDEX

INDEX

206

INDEX

Taverner, Captain, 67
TB hospital, Point Edward, 143
Telecommunications, 78–81
Telephones, 78–80
Television channels, 187
T. G. Shaughnessy (tanker), 73, *123*
Three Sisters, 152
Tompkins, Father Jimmy, 101–2, 137, *142*
Tompkins Memorial Library, Reserve, 138
Tompkinsville, 101
Tourism, 112, 115–17
Tourist accommodation, 117, 176, 177–9
Tourist publications, 177, 187
Townshend, Gregory, 49
Towns Incorporation Act (1888), 125
Toyota, 112
Trailer sites, 178
TransCanada Highway, 26, 75, 81, 83, 86, 173, 174, 182
Trawlers, 92
Treasure, 169–71
Treaty of Paris (1763), 48, 90
Treaty of Utrecht (1713), 43, 150
Trossachs, 152
Trout, 37
Trout River, 73
Troy, 113
Truro, 172
Tuna, 37–8

U-boat, 67
Uisge Bhan Falls Walking Trail, 176
Ukrainians, 157
Uniacke, Richard, Jr, 32, 53, 54
Union of Nova Scotia Indians, 148–9
Union Presbyterian Church, Albert Bridge, *88*, 158
Union Telephone Company, 79
United Church, 163
United Empire Loyalists, 157
United Maritime Fishermen, 100–1
Universe Japan (tanker), 73
'Upper Canada', 103
Uranium, 113–14
Urban Service Area, 127

Vauban, Sébastien, Marquis de, 43
Vegetation, 24, 30–12
Verrier, Colonel, 43
Verville, 43
Victoria County, 20, 24, 31, 40, 84, 86, 125, 126, 134, 135, 137, 138, 143; population, 12, 94, 118ff
Vieuxport, Father de, 158

Vimont, Father, 158
Vinland, 40

Walking Trails, 176–7, 183–4
Warner, Charles Dudley, 116
War of 1812, 13, 157
Warren, Commodore, 45
Warren Lake, 19
Washabuck, 38, 64, 130
Weather, 24–30
Welfare services, 129–31
Wentworth Park, 36
West Arichat, 64
West Bay, 84, 127
'West Indian Cricket Club', 157
West Indians, 157
Westmount, 120, 174
Wheat, 94
White Hill, 17
White pine, 96
White spruce, 24, 30, 96
Whitney, Henry Melville, 59
Whitney Pier, 129, 131, 157, 164
Whitney Pier Neighbourhood Action Committee, 130
Whycocomagh, 13, 26, 64, 74, 80, 83, 117, 120, 147, 155, 157, 162, 163, 175, 176
Whycocomagh Indian Reserve, 148
Wigwam, 39
'Wild Archie', 65
Wild life, 32, 35–8
William Tell (ship), 54
Willow ptarmigan, 36
Wilmot, Governor Montagu, 48
Wire birch, 24, 30, 31
Witchcraft, 165–6
Wolfall, Master, 158
Wolfe, James, 47–8
Wood-lot owners, 96
Woodworking industries, 97
World War I, 103, 107, 157
World War II, 103, 107
Wreck Cove, 13
Wright, Orville, 76
Wynyard, Lt George, 166–7
'Wynyard Ghost Story', 166–7

Xavier College, 136

Yacht Clubs, 174
Yarmouth, 75, 172
Yellow birch, 30
York, Duke of, 58–9
Yorke, Lt-Col John, 50, 167
Youth Hostels, 178